SCOTLAND'S CASTLES

HISTORIC SCOTLAND

SCOTLAND'S CASTLES

CHRIS TABRAHAM

B. T. Batsford Ltd / Historic Scotland

© Chris Tabraham 1997
First published 1997

Typeset by Bernard Cavender Design & Greenwood Graphics Publishing
and printed by The Bath Press, Bath

Published by B T Batsford Ltd
583 Fulham Road, London SW6 5BY

A CIP catalogue record for this book is
available from the British Library.

ISBN 0 7134 7965 5 (limp)
0 7134 8147 1 (cased)

Front cover
Kilchurn Castle on Loch Awe, Argyllshire, with the snow-
capped peak of Beinn Eunaich behind. One of the most
photographed of all Scotland's castles, Kilchurn served as
the principal residence of the Campbells of Glenorchy (later
the earls of Breadalbane) for over 200 years from 1450. In
the twilight of its days, the 1690s, it was fitted out as a
barracks for the first earl's private army (Historic Scotland).

Back cover
A gruesome stone face from Caerlaverock Castle,
Dumfriesshire. Now on display in the visitor centre, it was
doubtless once placed in a prominent position on the castle
walls, silently threatening those who might disturb Lord
Maxwell's peace (Historic Scotland).

Contents

Illustrations

44 Cardoness Castle, Kirkcudbrightshire: the tower house in 1475   79

45 Crichton Castle, Midlothian, in 1400   80

46 Smailholm Tower, Roxburghshire, in 1475   81

47 Woodcut showing cooking in a lord's hall in 1500   82

48 Affleck Castle, Angus   83

49 Affleck Castle: the chapel   84

50 Orchardton Tower, Kirkcudbrightshire   85

51 Borthwick Castle and Church, Midlothian, from the air   86

52 Borthwick Castle: floor plans   87

53 Borthwick Castle: the great hall   88

54 Bothwell Castle from the air   90

55 Dirleton Castle: the storage vaults   90

56 Crichton Castle in 1450   91

57 Crichton Castle: the entrance to Chancellor Crichton's great hall   92

58 Mearns Castle, Renfrewshire   94

59 Craigmillar Castle, Edinburgh: the machicolated curtain wall   94

60 Lochranza Castle, Arran: the box-machicolation over the front door   95

61 Threave Castle: the central gun tower in 1455   97

62 Newark Castle, Renfrewshire: the gatehouse   98

63 Ravenscraig Castle, Fife   99

64 Dunbar Castle, East Lothian, from the air   100

65 Dunbar Castle blockhouse: plan   101

66 Craignethan Castle, Lanarkshire: the caponier   103

67 Craignethan Castle: inside the caponier in 1540   104

68 Eyemouth Fort, Berwickshire, from the air   106

69 Dirleton Castle: gunholed window   107

70 Tolquhon Castle, Aberdeenshire: gatehouse   108

71 St Andrews Castle: plan of the mine and countermine   109

72 Cardinal David Beaton   110

73 St Andrews Castle: the mine   110

74 Edzell Castle, Angus: the tower house   112

75 Edzell Castle in 1600   113

76 Melgund Castle, Angus, in 1550   114

77 Statue of a crossbowman from the palace at Stirling Castle   115

78 Huntly Castle, Aberdeenshire   116

79 Huntly Castle: the palace floor plans   119

80 Carsluith Castle, Kirkcudbrightshire   120

81 Ballencrieff Castle, East Lothian: window drawbar   121

82 Claypotts Castle, Angus: the hall in 1590   122

83 Slacks Tower, Roxburghshire   123

84 Plan of Slacks farm   124

85 Glenochar bastel-house, Lanarkshire   125

86 Monea Castle, County Fermanagh   128

87 Leslie Castle, Aberdeenshire   129

Colour plates

Acknowledgements

I am very grateful to those who have helped me with this book: my colleagues David Breeze and Doreen Grove for their invaluable comments, David Simon, Harry Bland and Tom Borthwick for their reconstruction illustrations, and David Henrie and Mike Brooks for their photographs. I am also indebted to the following individuals and institutions for their kind permission to reproduce material: His Grace the Duke of Roxburghe (1), Gordon Ewart (9), Roger Miket (13), Peter Yeoman (27), Iain MacIvor (65), Tam Ward (85), Department of the Environment, Northern Ireland (86), John Knight (87), the Royal Commission on the Ancient and Historical Monuments of Scotland (37, 39, 40, 58 and 84), the City of Carlisle (30), the National Museums of Scotland (31) and colour plate 10, the National Trust for Scotland (35) and the Royal Scottish Geographical Society (2). All the remaining illustrations are Crown Copyright: Historic Scotland. I must also thank the many unsung archaeological heroes who have endured the vagaries of the Scottish climate to shed more light on the history of Scotland's castles. Finally, I owe a special debt to Stewart Cruden, whose work *The Scottish Castle* remains the standard textbook on the subject, and whose compendious knowledge and infectious enthusiasm for castles rubbed off on so many folk, including me.

Introduction: 'Welcvm freindis'

On a cold winter's evening a few years ago Jock Smith, a gap-toothed, bow-legged figure of a man, was preparing to lock up his premises for the night before making his way home. 'Auld Jock' was custodian for the Ministry of Public Building and Works of Threave Castle, the island fastness of the Black Douglases in the Galloway Dee. Having done his rounds of the grim, forbidding tower he was about to put the heavy iron key into the lock when he heard a deep voice call out from the bowels of the building: 'Jock, Jock', the disembodied voice pronounced, 'this is Archibald the Grim; an' it's just thee and me here noo.' Quick as a flash, Jock replied: 'O no it's not, ya bugger; I'm off!' In an instant the door was locked and Jock was rowing like a man possessed across the icy waters of the Dee to the safety of the far bank.

Those of us who have had the good fortune to visit Threave Island will have every sympathy for Jock; I suspect that we would all have done likewise had we been in his shoes – the ruined castle has a haunting quality, enough to make the hairs on the back of your neck stand on end. I know I would have turned and run, but I also know that I would have bitterly regretted it for the rest of my days. Who among us has not made a secret wish to go back in time, just for a short while, to see for ourselves exactly what life was like at a particular moment? What I would have given to have spent that winter's evening in the company of Black Archibald, third earl of the house of Douglas, lord of Galloway, scourge of the English and arguably the most powerful nobleman in the land at his death at Threave on Christmas Eve 1400. What he could have told me about castles and castle life; and what a book I might have written! As things are, this book of mine will just have to take its place alongside the others on the subject written by folk without the benefit of time travel.

Scotland is a land full of castles. Those two great Scottish castellologists, David MacGibbon and Thomas Ross, included 769 castles in their pioneering five-volume epic *The castellated and domestic architecture of Scotland from the twelfth to the eighteenth century*, published just over a century ago – and they confined their coverage to just stone ones. Today's computer in the National Monuments Record of Scotland holds thousands of entries covering all manner of medieval fortified sites, whether of stone or timber. Clearly, my book cannot include them all, nor would I wish it to. A simple gazetteer would not even begin to reveal the fascinating and complex story of Scotland's castles.

Scotland is also a country as rich as any other in its variety of castles. Folk in medieval times referred to them by a befuddling variety of names, among them *castrum, fortalicium, turris, manerium, mansio, domus, locus, palatium, capitale* and *principale messuagium*. I am sure that Black Archibald would have been able to enlighten me as to their respective meanings. However, all we can say today is that Scotland's castles came in all shapes and sizes – mighty castles royal, impressive seats of the great and grand, fortified homes of the middling sort and poky dwellings of those on the bottom rung of the landholding ladder. Clearly, this book should try to embrace them all, and I hope that it does. Only by looking at the Scottish fortified house in all its manifestations can we begin to appreciate the whole picture. The only conscious omission I make is the Scottish palace, which is to be the subject of a companion volume in this series.

There is an old adage: 'An Englishman's home is his castle.' Perhaps we should create another: 'A Scotsman's castle is his home.' In a sense this would be the more true aphorism for the medieval castle dominated Scottish life for far longer than was the case south of the Border.

What is more, we today have come to see castles as high-status sites, associating their ruins with the high-born in society. But this is to overlook just how many Scots from all walks of life, freeman or serf, towndweller or countryman, were dependent on the castle; it could be their home, their place of work, their place of worship, their rent office, their army barracks, their law court, their prison, their hotel, their place of entertainment – even their place of execution. As an archaeologist I am fascinated by this human aspect of the Scottish castle and this is what I attempt to cover in this book.

And so, as a carved lintel above the front door into Otterston Castle, Fife, declares:

1

Castles in the land: the twelfth century

When the queen heard this [news of her husband's death] she shrived, and devoutly took the Communion in church; and, commending herself unto God in prayer, she gave back her saintly soul to heaven, in the Castle of Maidens [Edinburgh] on 16th November, the fourth day after the king. Whereupon Donald Bane, the king's brother, having heard of her death, invaded the kingdom, at the head of a numerous band, and in hostilewise besieged the castle, where he knew the king's rightful and lawful heirs were. But, forasmuch as that spot is in itself strongly fortified by nature, he thought that the gates only should be guarded, because it was not easy to see any other entrance or outlet. When those who were within understood this, they brought down her holy body by a postern on the western side.

Origins

The moving story of the saintly Queen Margaret's death in Edinburgh Castle (**colour plate 1**) in November 1093, while in mourning for her beloved husband King Malcolm III, appears at first sight to give us our first mention of a Scottish castle in the country's annals. On further inspection, however, we discover that the author of the account, the chronicler John of Fordun, was writing in the later fourteenth century, almost three centuries after the tragic events, and that the near-contemporary recording of the event by Bishop Turgot in his

Life of St Margaret makes no mention of a castle, let alone one called the 'Castle of Maidens' at Edinburgh.

The nature of Queen Margaret's residence, whether at Edinburgh, Dunfermline or elsewhere, is only glimpsed at in Turgot's *Life*. He writes of churches and oratories, of private chambers, and of royal halls big enough to hold '300 poor people'. But nowhere does he mention castles. His descriptions could just as equally fit the remains of Dark Age buildings recently excavated on the rocky summits at Cruggleton (Wigtownshire) and Dundonald (Ayrshire), or beside the cliff-edge in Dunbar (East Lothian), and on the slope of wind-swept Doon Hill, a short distance inland from there. So were there castles in the land in Queen Margaret's day?

There were certainly castles south of the Border in England and Wales and across the North Sea on the mainland of Europe in her day. The origin of castles remains a mystery, but the debate need not concern us unduly for by the time castles appeared in Scotland they had developed a recognized form and function. Castles were essentially fortified residences of lordship, the homes of those who held land in return for military service. They might differ in size and scale according to the rank of those building and occupying them, and royal castles in particular served a heightened political and public role; but all castles essentially performed the same purpose.

It is just possible that Queen Margaret was personally acquainted with the castle form through her residence in England prior to her flight to Scotland in about 1070. Her husband Malcolm must surely have been familiar with them through his various forays into England. In 1092, the year the English king William Rufus captured Carlisle from the Scots and began to build a castle there, Malcolm journeyed to Gloucester Castle where he was snubbed by Rufus. Infuriated, Malcolm returned home and in the following year led his fourth and final raid into northern England. His ensuing death at the hand of Arkil Morel, one of Rufus's Norman knights, which led so soon after to Queen Margaret's demise, occurred within a bow-shot of Alnwick Castle.

Despite this intermittent friction between Malcolm's Scotland and Norman England, the two countries shared in a reasonably peaceful coexistence. This was further cemented after Margaret and Malcolm's deaths by arranged marriages and other amicable relationships between the two royal houses. In 1100 their elder daughter, Matilda, actually became queen of England when she wed William I's youngest son, Henry I; the Conqueror's invasion of Scotland in 1072, when he got as far as the River Tay and received King Malcolm's homage, must have been a fading memory at the wedding reception!

The increasing contact between the Scots and their new aristocratic neighbours inevitably brought the former into contact with all manner of French customs and ways. (The 'Norman' conquerors of England were drawn from a wider field than just Normandy, including regions like Brittany and the Pas de Calais.) We know that the temptation to imitate some of these habits was irresistible. Indeed, Donald Bane's seizure of the throne immediately after Queen Margaret's death, mentioned in Fordun's account, was said to have been motivated by his burning desire to rid the country of these incomers and their alien ways. These certainly included the introduction of mailed knights;

even King Macbeth in the early 1050s had had Normans in his retinue. But did these French ways also include the building of castles?

It is difficult not to see them including this most visible form of aristocratic power, although the evidence is scanty to say the least and no castle site has yet been positively identified as dating from this period. King Edgar, the second of Margaret and Malcolm's six sons (and the one who broke the tragic news of his father's death to his mother), certainly received substantial help from William Rufus in his successful attempt to overthrow Donald Bane in 1097; and among those who came north in that year to serve him was an English baron called Robert, son of Godwin. Following the victory, Edgar rewarded Robert with an estate in Lothian, close to the English Border, where the latter endeavoured to build himself a castle.

This may be an isolated incident, the exception perhaps to prove the rule that castles were not yet part of Scottish society or a feature in her landscape. But given the close ties between the Canmores and the Conqueror's dynasty, and given also the undoubted familiarity of the Scots with the new-fangled fighting ways of the Normans, it is difficult to resist the notion that the castle might have become a little more firmly embedded in the fabric of Scotland prior to the time of King David I in the second quarter of the twelfth century.

There is some evidence that King Alexander I (1107–24) was beginning to rely less on foreign mercenaries and more on those who would settle permanently and offer military service in return for their lands. The building of castles would be the logical consequence of such a policy. Even if the incomers were not building castles, it would be surprising if the king himself, having seen the new strongholds built by the English crown at the likes of Carlisle and Newcastle, was not persuaded to follow suit. One wonders what might have stood atop the rocky crags of Stirling or Edinburgh in the early twelfth century. The documents are all exhausted; only archaeological excavation can solve the puzzle – perhaps.

David – king of the castle

King David I, the youngest of Margaret and Malcolm's six sons, succeeded his brother Alexander in 1124 (**1**). He had, however, been in effective control of southern Scotland from as early as 1113. It was during the time of David, 'that most vigorous and courteous of kings', that the process of settling an immigrant aristocracy on Scotland's soil began in earnest, a development that was to continue long after his death in 1153 (under the encouragement of his two grandsons who succeeded him, Malcolm IV 'the Maiden' and William 'the Lion') and which cannot be deemed to have

been completed until William's demise in 1214. A verse inserted into the *Chronicle of Melrose* for the year 1153 leaves us in no doubt about his contribution:

> David was king in Scotland for twenty-nine years,
> Warily discerning what was provident;
> After he had fortified the kingdom with castles and arms,
> The king died, an old man, at Carlisle.

Fordun himself proudly proclaimed: 'He it is that has decked thee [Scotland] with castles and towns, and with lofty towers.'

David was born in Dunfermline about 1080. While still in his teens, he travelled south into England for his sister Matilda's wedding to Henry I. There he remained for the next decade and more, attending at the English court and observing at first hand French ways and customs. He became one of Henry's barons, and in 1113 he married Maud, a rich widow,

1 David I, King of Scots (1124–1153), with his grandson and successor (right), King Malcolm IV (1153–65); a decorated initial from a charter of 1159 granted to Kelso Abbey, Roxburghshire.

thereby becoming lord of the extensive Honour of Huntingdon, in the East Midlands. Shortly afterwards, he returned to the land of his birth with a Norman education, a Norman wife and a large English estate full of Norman knights. Life in Scotland was never going to be quite the same again.

David's legacy for Scotland, continued by his grandsons, was immense. He reorganized the church and introduced the new reformed monastic orders; he established towns and built mints for the striking of coin; he introduced a new type of sheriffdom based on the Norman model; and he forced the pace on the 'feudalizing' of Scotland, encouraging newcomers to settle in the land and cajoling native lords to adapt to the new ways. One thing is certain, it must have been 'boom time' for the construction industry, and alongside the new cathedrals, the monasteries, the parish churches and the towns arose the castles, the most potent symbol of the new order.

Castles for kings, barons and knights

There were essentially two categories of castle introduced into Scotland during the course of the twelfth century: royal castles and castles built by tenants of the crown, barons and knights, holding their land in return for military service.

By 1200 there were royal castles as far apart as Berwick-upon-Tweed, hard by the English Border, Ayr in the west and Dunskeath in the north. These were intended to perform a variety of functions. They were primarily, of course, the fortified residences of the monarchy, though the royal family never dwelt in them permanently but travelled around the kingdom, overseeing the nation's affairs, consuming their rents which were normally paid in kind, or simply pursuing their leisure interests. While in residence, the royal family ruled from them, entertained at them, and lived and died in them. Prince Henry, David's only son and heir, tragically died in the royal castle at Peebles (2) in 1152, King David himself passed away at Carlisle Castle in the following year, Malcolm breathed his last at

Jedburgh Castle in 1165 and William his last at Stirling Castle in 1214.

In addition to their use as occasional residences, royal castles were important as permanent centres of national government. Each in effect became the regional headquarters of the royal administrative unit – the shire or sheriffdom – whose chief administrator was the sheriff. The sheriff usually served also as the constable, or keeper of the castle, being responsible for its garrisoning, provisioning and maintenance. He had an official residence in the castle and held his court of justice in its great hall. Royal castles were thus law courts and prisons as well as residences.

The incoming aristocracy, and the native nobility who embraced the new order, also built castles. There were several rungs on the landholding ladder, and no doubt their fortified residences reflected this gradation. At the top were the magnates, who moved in much the same circle as the king himself; quite a number must have been his close personal friends. They were expected to control and administer their large estates and from them draw the necessary military strength required by the crown.

Typical of the incoming magnates was Robert de Brus, ancestor of King Robert the Bruce, who was granted the vast lordship of Annandale, adjacent to the English Border, in 1124 in return for the service of ten knights. De Brus was already lord of Cleveland, in England, but his roots reached back to Normandy, to the village of Brix in the Cotentin. The castle that Robert de Brus built beside the river at Annan (Dumfriesshire), which still partly exists, was not only his fortified residence but the estate office and courthouse as well. An example of a native baron adapting to the changed regime is Earl Duncan of Fife, descended from the ancient mormaers who governed north of the Forth in the pre-feudal age. About 1136 Duncan was granted the earldom as a fief in return for military service, and the castle at Cupar (Fife) was probably built by him as a consequence of this new-found status.

2 Peebles Castle and burgh, from Armstrong's plan of
1775. By this date the castle hill was being used as a
bowling green, but its pivotal position, at the junction of the
Peebles Water with the River Tweed and at the end of the
High Street, is clear enough. The present parish church at
the east end of the castle hill is the successor to the castle
chapel where, in 1152, King David I instituted a perpetual
chantry for the soul of his son, Earl Henry, who is thought
to have died in the castle in June of that year.

Magnates like Earl Duncan and Robert de
Brus held their large lordships directly of the
crown, but in order to meet their obligations
they had to grant smaller parcels of land to
others in return for service. These lower-ranking
landholders were called knights, and they too
were empowered to build castles. A good
instance of this is the great feudal lordship of
the Stewarts, concentrated chiefly in the west of

17

the country and administered from their two principal castles at Renfrew and Dundonald. Only a comparatively small part of the lordship was held 'in demesne' (that is, retained in the lord's hands); the greater portion was let as subordinate fiefs to a variety of tenants and vassals, to men like Robert Croc, knight in Crookston (Glasgow), and Gilbert fitz Richer, knight in Tarbolton (Ayrshire). In each of these two fiefs there is an early castle (**3**).

The word 'demesne' survives today as 'mains', meaning the home farm of an estate cultivated by or for the proprietor. There are two other place-names, *ingleston* and *boreland*, which indicate the former existence of a castle,

sometimes where there is no sign of one today. 'Ingleston' implies a settlement of incoming Englishmen in the area, while 'boreland' (sometimes 'bordland' or 'borland') referred to land that provided food for the lord's board or table. The farm-name of Borlum, on the high ground overlooking Urquhart Castle beside Loch Ness (Inverness-shire), is another corruption of the word.

The nature of castles – the literary evidence

What form then did these royal, baronial and knightly castles take? To help us in our quest we have the evidence from literature, from physical remains and from excavation.

There is the most wonderful love-story surviving from late twelfth-century Scotland, the *Roman de Fergus*, written by Guillaume le Clerc, identified by one authority (D.D.R. Owen in his translation *Fergus of Galloway, Knight of*

3 Crookston Castle, Glasgow. The tower-house residence of Sir John Stewart of Darnley, built about 1400, stands within a ringwork defence dating to Sir Robert Croc's time in the later twelfth century.

King Arthur, 1991) as William Malveisin, a royal clerk who rose to become bishop of St Andrews in 1202. His romance, written perhaps in honour of the wedding of Roland of Galloway and Elena de Morville about the year 1170, is a novel worthy of the Booker prize! But despite being a work of fiction, with its predilection for tales of knightly derring-do, it paints for us today a unique and utterly fascinating picture of contemporary life in southern Scotland in this feudal age; and the picture is positively brimming with castles.

Our eponymous hero first encounters his true-love, Galiena, at her uncle's castle, Liddel. We read of the bridge below the castle gate, of the stable where his horse was well supplied with hay and oats, and of the steps leading to the main hall, 'which was by no means small' and was furnished with couches and trestle-tables fashioned from ebony. A visit to present-day Liddel Castle, atop a steep cliff overlooking Liddel Water in deepest Liddesdale (Roxburghshire), is made the more rewarding with a copy of the *Roman de Fergus* to hand. It is a motte-and-bailey castle of somewhat eccentric form which in reality was the residence of Ranulf de Soules, who held the fief of Great Doddington (Northamptonshire) on King David's Honour of Huntingdon but who came north when the king granted him the lordship of Liddesdale and probably also the office of butler in his household. His nephew, the younger Ranulf, who succeeded him, became the stuff of legend in his own right as 'the wicked Lord Soules' who in 1207 was murdered in his castle at Liddel by his own servants.

Another absorbing insight from the *Roman* comes with Fergus's arrival at the 'Castle of the Dark Rock' high up in a mountain near Melrose, the 'wonderfully powerful stronghold' of a wicked giant whom Fergus, after a great deal of difficulty, overpowers and slays. Wearily he enters the castle where the dead giant's maidens 'provide for him a splendid, excellent bath' in the hall in the keep whose pillars hang

'with more than 1000 shields, hauberks, helmets, and all the gear for arming a knight'. We read also of a great hall separate from the keep, of an 'out-of-the way cellar' wherein was a handsome horse, and of the drawbridge over the moat. At one point Fergus climbs to the upper floor of the keep and looks out of the window where he regards 'the tilled and the uncultivated land' of Lothian and the castle of Roxburgh (see **32**), where his lover is besieged. We subsequently discover that this castle has a square keep 'some 180 feet [55m] above the ground', a church and a postern gate.

But the most revealing insight comes at the very beginning of the tale as Fergus sets out on his travels from the home of his father, Soumillet:

> On the road out of Galloway, in a castle down a valley, lived a peasant of Pelande very close to the Irish Sea. He had his dwelling splendidly situated on a great rock, encircled by clay and wattle walls. The hill was topped by a tower that was not made of granite or limestone: its wall was built high of earth, with ramparts and battlements. The peasant was very well off to have such a handsome home by the sea. If he looked out he could see for thirty leagues all round. Nobody inside could feel threatened by any maker of siege equipment or from any assault, the rock being high and massive. Without a word of a lie, the peasant governed and held in his possession the whole of the country which had been his for a very long time, and nobody could take it from him.

There are two likely candidates for Soumillet's residence, Kirkclaugh Motte near Anwoth (Kirkcudbrightshire) and Cruggleton near Garlieston (**4**). The latter is the more probable given its known association with the ancient lords of Galloway and we are fortunate that excavations have been carried out there recently to complement the evidence from literature (see pages 26–7).

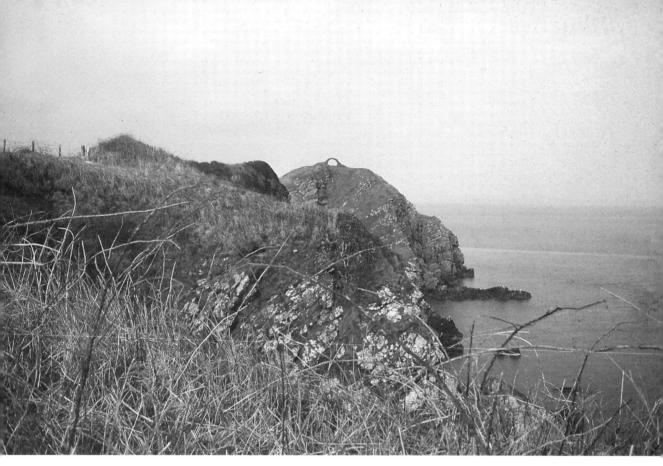

4 Cruggleton Castle (centre background), near Garlieston, Wigtownshire, perched on a rocky cliff overlooking Wigtown Bay. The arch on the summit once formed part of the later medieval castle.

The nature of castles – the physical evidence

The most characteristic type of early castle is the motte. The word 'motta' literally means 'a clod of earth' but from the twelfth century it was used to denote a castle mound, whether natural or man-made. There are several depictions of mottes on the Bayeux Tapestry, that splendid late eleventh-century strip-cartoon telling the story of the Norman conquest of England. One of them, that at Dol in Brittany, was the castle of the steward of the bishop of Dol, from whom our own Stewart dynasty of kings and queens was descended. Fieldwork in Scotland has identified about 300 of these motte castles, of varying shape and size. To illustrate them I shall take two examples, each quite different, from opposite ends of the country.

The motte-and-bailey castle known as the Bass of Inverurie, in the Garioch of Aberdeenshire, is one of the best preserved in Scotland; it is also one of the best documented (5). It lies today in a quiet cemetery to the south-east of the present town, sandwiched between the rivers Urie and Don, but in its day it was the focal point of the burgh established by Earl David of Huntingdon in the late twelfth century; the burgh is on record by 1195 and the castle by 1199.

The motte and bailey suffered from some landscaping in the nineteenth century but it is essentially intact. It appears to be entirely man-made. The motte, the Bass itself, has the classic conical shape, like an upside-down pudding bowl, and rises some 15m (49ft) above the surrounding ground. The summit area is about 18m (59ft) in diameter. The bailey, or Little Bass, now shrouded in trees, is both smaller in height and in summit area. There is now no hint of the defensive ditch which doubtless encircled both motte and bailey, though excavation in the nineteenth century unearthed remains of an oak bridge.

Earl David (1152–1219), the builder of the Bass, was a member of the royal family, the youngest of King David's three grandsons. Following the death in 1165 of his eldest brother, Malcolm, David was heir-apparent to the throne until 1198. He was thus among the elite in society, moving in the highest circles. During his thirties, Earl David acquired vast estates, in England as well as in Scotland. As earl of Huntingdon, David was lord of a greater part of the English East Midlands. The Garioch, his main holding in Scotland, covered about 260sq km (100sq miles) between the outskirts of Aberdeen in the south-east and Strathbogie (now Huntly) in the north-west. He had other estates, including those in and around Dundee, but his life was largely spent at his two chief castles, at Fotheringay (Northamptonshire) and Inverurie. Today, Fotheringay is much better known in connection with another Scottish royal, Mary Queen of Scots, who was executed there in 1587.

The contrast between the impressive Bass of Inverurie and the humble motte castle at Barmagachan, near Borgue in Kirkcudbrightshire, could not be greater. Unlike the Bass, but like a considerable number of Scottish mottes, Barmagachan is not an artificial mound but has been created from a natural rocky outcrop (**colour plate 2**). The circular, steep-sided mound has a rock-cut ditch around its base, stands 6m (20ft) high and has a summit area measuring 17m (56ft) across. There is, though, no trace of an accompanying bailey, a feature which Barmagachan shares with many Scottish mottes. It is hard to see the motte alone serving all the needs of its lord, particularly one measuring just 17m (56ft) across, and we may assume that some form of outer enclosure existed, though not necessarily one raised above the ground. At Southwick Motte, in eastern Kirkcudbrightshire, aerial photography hints at

5 The Bass of Inverurie, Aberdeenshire, the Scottish residence of Earl David of Huntingdon, and a classic example of a motte-and-bailey castle.

an enclosed but unelevated area beside the motte itself, and at the Motte of Montfode, close to Ardrossan (Ayrshire), excavation revealed the existence of two outer ditches which, although of unknown date, may conceivably have been part of the bailey defence.

We know neither when Barmagachan was built nor who built it. We assume a twelfth- or early thirteenth-century date, though the lesson of Roberton (Lanarkshire) serves to caution us about making such statements in the absence of excavation (see page 64). The builder could either have been an incomer (the place-name Ingleston occurs nearby) – and a recent reassessment proposes Bernard de Ripley, from the north of England, in about 1235 – or a native Gallovidian. Either way, it is reasonable to assume from the physical remains at Barmagachan that its owner was not in the same league as Earl David of Huntingdon.

One puzzle about these Scottish mottes is their distribution throughout the country. Although there are examples in east-central Scotland, in the Lothians, in Fife and north of the River Tay, the vast majority are clustered in areas which in the twelfth and early thirteenth centuries were on the periphery of the realm and which posed real problems for the monarchy, regions like Galloway and Moray. The obvious conclusion to be drawn is that motte castles were more likely to be built in districts where political unrest was a distinct possibility. This was after all how the motte castle probably originated, as a quick and comparatively cheap solution to providing a lord with the necessary security against attack. It has been estimated that an average-sized motte, 5m (16ft) high and 15m (50ft) across at the top, would have taken fifty people about forty working days (assuming a ten-hour day) to construct. All they needed were their muscles, their digging tools and a good site foreman; only the joinery work required specialist skills.

There were certainly forms of castle other than mottes in Scotland, and contrary to modern perception, the motte was probably the exception rather than the rule. After all, much of the country was relatively peaceful and the incoming lords managed, by and large, to settle their new estates without much difficulty. Take Freskin, for example, a Fleming who came to Scotland late in King David's reign. He clearly felt insecure in his estate in Moray as his mighty motte-and-bailey castle at Duffus, near Elgin, demonstrates; the rebellion of the men of Moray, ruthlessly put down by King David in 1130, must have been a factor in Freskin's decision to build in such a formidable manner. But before moving north to Moray, Freskin was already settled in Lothian, as lord of Strathbrock, near Livingston. Today there is no trace of his lowland castle, and although it is just possible that it may have been a motte castle which has not survived, it is far more likely that it was something less robustly built but just as serviceable as his lordly residence. So what were the alternatives open to Freskin?

We know both from documentary evidence and through fieldwork that islands, whether in rivers or lochs, were used for lordly residences. Uchtred of Galloway was murdered at his island fastness in the River Dee, possibly Threave, in 1174. The landscape of medieval Scotland for the most part was altogether more boggy than it appears today and there was thus a greater opportunity to exploit the terrain to this end. Islands had an innate defensive quality requiring little more than an encircling wall of wood or stone to make them reasonably secure. They might be naturally occurring islands or man-made constructions called crannogs, like the two in Lochrutton Loch (Kirkcudbrightshire), one of which has been recently dated by dendrochronology to the late twelfth or thirteenth century (6).

Perhaps the most common form of castle, though, was the one where the castle area remained on the same level as the surrounding ground but which was defended by a raised earthen bank fronted by a ditch. Archaeologists have christened these 'ringworks'. They were

N

157
128
127
133
116
90
171
124
91
94
244
123
39
253
36
42
40
28
18
17
59
37
60
160
33
61
54
75
71
197
196

Phase 2 : Hall

Phase 2 : Palisade

Phase 3 : Tower

Phase 3 : Extended Hall

0   5 metres

impressive drinking-hall next to the church. Recent excavations there have uncovered beside the upstanding ruin of the church the remains of a large building which may be the 'drinking-hall' referred to. The saga evidence for undefended homesteads is corroborated by archaeological evidence at such sites as Jarlshof, at the southern tip of Shetland, where at no point in the period of Norse occupation from the ninth through to the thirteenth century is there any hint of fortification.

Where strongholds are specifically referred to they are described either as borgs or castles, but the distinction, if any, is not readily apparent. It may be that the saga writer meant 'borg' to imply a stronghold of some antiquity and 'castle' a new type of defensive building. Certainly 'Moseyjarborg', the borg in Hjaltland (Shetland) where Erlend Ungi 'made great preparations for defence' against Earl Harald Maddadson in 1155, is the well-known Mousa Broch built about 1,000 years earlier. A borg in Caithness, Lambaborg, seems also to be a place of last resort, a retreat for Swein and his companions from the murdering Margad. It is described as 'a strong place ... situated on a sea-girt rock, and on the landward side there was a well-built stone wall', which conjures up a picture of a late prehistoric promontory fort rather than a medieval castle.

By contrast, the references to castles imply new structures. Four castles in the region are specifically referred to in the *Saga* – one on the island of Damsay, another on Wyre, a third in Kirkwall, and the fourth at Thurso in Caithness. It is the castle on Wyre that is of the greatest interest because the saga writer's description is complemented by the physical remains of the castle itself.

Of Cubbie Roo and other towers

Cubbie Roo's Castle stands on the crest of a ridge at the north end of the tiny island of Wyre. Close by is the ruined twelfth-century St Mary's Church and the modern farm name, the Bu of Wyre, recalls the great Norse drinking-hall that

would have preceded the stone castle as the family residence, and quite possibly continued in use alongside the new castle. The saga writer tells us that about the year 1150 Kolbein Hruga, the young man who lived in the island, 'built a fine stone castle, which was a strong defence'. Kubbie was a Norse nickname for Kolbein; hence the corruption of his name to Cubbie Roo.

Kolbein Hruga's castle consisted of a small stone tower, 7m (23ft) square, over walls almost 2m (6ft) thick. All that exists today is the lower part of the basement storey. There is no ground-floor entrance and this cellar must have been reached by a ladder from the first floor. The only features are two slit windows and a water tank sunk into the ground. The original height of the tower is impossible to determine, but three storeys would have given reasonably clear views across Gairsay Sound (**10**). The outer defences around the tower were subsequently abandoned and built over, but excavation has shown that the original fortified area, measuring 29 by 23m (95 by 75ft), was protected by a 2m (6ft) deep flat-bottomed ditch with a stout stone wall on the inner lip and a low earthen rampart along the counterscarp.

The building of castles by the Norsemen may at first sight seem surprising. Although they came from the same root as the Normans, by the twelfth century their social and political culture was very different from that of their southern kinsmen. But this is to ignore the remarkable degree of contact between the men from the north and the rest of the known world. Two examples will suffice to illustrate this. King Sigurd Magnusson, who succeeded to the throne of Norway in 1103 following his father's death in Ireland, set out on a pilgrimage to Jerusalem in 1107 which took him the best part of three years to accomplish; his people gave him his by-name 'the Jorsala-farer' on his return. And the *Orkneyinga Saga* recounts in fascinating detail Earl Rognvald's three-year voyage on crusade to the Holy Land in the 1150s. Such voyages must inevitably have brought the Norsemen into contact with the new-fangled castles; indeed, the

10 An impression of Cubbie Roo's castle, on Wyre, Orkney, as it might have looked in 1231 when the assassins of Earl John Haraldson sought refuge there and held out against the earl's avenging friends. On the right is the little late twelfth-century church, and in the background the Bu of Wyre, with its great feasting hall. Drawn by David Simon.

saga writer regales us with Rognvald's successful attack on a castle in Galicialand (modern Galicia in north-west Spain). The confrontation has everything: missiles raining down on both camps, boiling pitch and brimstone being poured from the battlements, and the piles of burning faggots melting the lime holding the castle walls together – all great stuff! Such encounters must have made an impression on the Norsemen. In the unsettled, blood-spattered society of the Northern Isles so excitingly depicted by the saga writer, there was surely a place for the castle.

The Norsemen's encounters with castles were not always hostile for there was peaceful contact with other nations, including Scotland. This included marriage alliances. Harald Maddadson, earl of Orkney from 1139 to 1206,

for example, had an Orcadian mother but his father was Matad, earl of Atholl. And when Harald himself married in about 1150, he took as his lady Affrica, daughter of Earl Duncan of Fife, the builder of Cupar Castle. It seems likely that Earl Harald was the builder of castles. The stone towers, or keeps, at Braal, near Thurso, and the Old Man of Wick (both Caithness), have both been credited to him. The latter lies on a narrow spine of rock projecting into the North Sea a little distance south of Wick town (11). The upstanding tower at the neck of the promontory has marked similarities with Cubbie Roo, like the lack of a ground-floor entrance and the narrow slit window lighting the basement. But the ruined shell of Old Wick rises much higher than Cubbie Roo, giving us further clues as to its appearance. It was entered at first-floor level and was entirely unvaulted throughout its four storeys, its wooden floors resting on ledges around the walls. The fireplaces did not have flues rising through the thickness of the walls but clay smoke-hoods attached to the inside faces. There is no evidence for either mural stairs or wall chambers, but the

11 The Castle of Old Wick ('the Old Man of Wick'), Caithness, from the air. The long, narrow promontory has been cut off from the hinterland by a rock-cut ditch The tall tower at the landward end overshadows an array of building foundations running the length of the promontory.

loss of most of one wall prevents us from saying whether such ever existed. Beyond the tower and spread out over the rest of the promontory are the foundations of stone buildings which presumably complemented the lord's accommodation within the keep.

The stone towers at Cubbie Roo, Braal and Old Wick stand in marked contrast to the contemporary castles built within the realm of Scotland, where the prevailing impression is one of earth and timber. But the abundance in Orkney and Caithness of good building stone for the mason, and the dearth of trees for the carpenter-joiner, must be chiefly responsible for this difference. Earl Harald's brother-in-law, Earl Duncan II of Fife, also built a great castle on his lordship of Strathbogie (subsequently renamed Huntly) in Aberdeenshire towards the end of the century. It was a motte-and-bailey castle, in the Norman tradition (see 78). But given the evidence we have from the *Roman de Fergus*, and from the excavations at Barton Hill, Cruggleton and elsewhere, who is to deny that, other than the choice of building materials, Earl Duncan's timber tower atop his motte at the Peel of Strathbogie was any different in form and function than Earl Harald's stone keep at Old Wick, or Kolbein Hruga's on Wyre.

2
A golden age of castles: the thirteenth century

Now they [the Norwegians] collected their force and their ships, about the islands; and they got eighty ships. And they sailed south round the Mull of Kintyre, and so in to Bute. The Scots sat there in the castle; and a certain steward was over the Scots. They proceeded to the castle, and made a hard assault on it, but the Scots defended themselves well, and they poured down upon them boiling pitch and lead. The Norwegians bound over themselves shields of wood, and they hewed the wall, because the stone was soft; and the wall fell down after that. The torch-bearer who was called Skagi shot the steward to death at the moment when he leapt upon the castle wall. They fought with the castle men for three days, before they won it. There they took much treasure, and one Scottish knight, who ransomed himself for 300 merks of refined silver.

When the west was won

The dramatic story of the Norwegian assault on the castle of the Steward of Scotland at Rothesay in 1230, related in *Eirspennill's Hakon Hakon's son's Saga*, is the earliest account we have of an assault on any Scottish castle. The action marked the beginning of the end for any claim to suzerainty the kings of Norway had over the western seaboard of Scotland, for although the northmen were successful in taking the castle on this occasion, they were compelled to withdraw shortly

afterwards. When King Hakon IV returned with an even bigger force thirty-three years later, and once again besieged and took the castle, he met with misfortune off the Ayrshire coast near Largs and withdrew to Kirkwall where, in the hall of the bishop's residence, he died two months later. The Treaty of Perth, signed by Hakon's successor, King Magnus, and the king of Scots, Alexander III, in 1266 effectively brought the lands and islands of the west under Scottish control. Scotland was about to enter a 'golden age'. It was certainly a golden age as far as castle building was concerned.

The besiegers of Rothesay Castle in 1230 were, in fact, headed not by a Norwegian but by Gillespec (Uspak in Norse) MacDougall, a grandson of Somerled. Somerled had spent a lifetime creating a great lordship stretching from Gigha in the south to the Uists in the north, playing one realm off against the other as well as beating off the predatory activities of the kings of Man, masters in the Outer Hebrides and quite possibly Skye also. Somerled's descendants, including the MacDougalls and the MacDonalds, built on his success. But they were not the only players in the field, for other families of Celtic stock made the most of the situation, like the MacSweens, the MacLachlans and the Lamonts. All were fiercely independent and proud of their roots, and they have given us a lasting treasure, one of the most marvellous collections of stone castles anywhere (**12**).

12 A depiction of a castle, possibly Dunvegan on Skye, on the tomb of Alasdair Crotach MacLeod, lord of Dunvegan (died 1547), in St Clement's Church, Rodel, Harris.

The rugged coastline of Argyllshire and western Inverness-shire is dotted about with castles. The vast majority belong to a later era (see **colour plate 14**), but among them is a group whose origins lie in this period when the west was won for Scotland. The history of fortification in the region, of course, reaches back much further, into the Iron Age, and the fact that many of the later castle sites have the prefix *dun*, generally meaning 'fortified hill' but which in this part of the country could equally describe a prehistoric broch or dun, suggests a continuity of fortified settlement of which the medieval castle was but the last in the sequence. Archaeological excavation has shown how Iron Age duns, like that at Dun Lagaigdh beside Loch Broom in Wester Ross, continued as fortified residences into the Middle Ages.

We now have no way of knowing just who the folk were who lived in Dun Lagaigdh in the

Middle Ages, or quite what their status in society was, although the discovery of a large coin hoard secreted there around 1230 suggests they were people of substance. Perhaps another site in the region holds a clue. Dun Ringill, hugging the cliff-edge overlooking Loch Slapin in the south-east of the Island of Skye, is so evidently a structure of Iron Age date – a near-circular, thick-walled drystone structure with one very narrow entrance passage complete with door-checks and bar-holes, and one intra-mural cell (**13**). However, two features betray the fact that this ancient fortress was still serving as a stronghold (a *borg* in the jargon of the saga writers) in the medieval period: a ditch around the outside and the foundations of two rectangular buildings within. Although Dun Ringill has a shadowy history, it is reputed to have been the traditional seat of the MacKinnon chiefs before they moved to Caisteal Maol at Kyleakin. Dun Ringill may well then be typical of the fortified residences of many of those holding maritime lordships across the western

13 Dun Ringill, beside Loch Slapin, on Skye, an Iron Age defensive structure refortified and reoccupied in the Middle Ages, probably by the clan chief of the MacKinnons.

seaboard in the thirteenth century. There were others, though, who were moved to build afresh in an alien tradition.

Castle Sween and the new curtain-walled castles

These new castles are characterized by high walls, which we today call curtain walls, enclosing areas of ground irregular in shape but normally rectilinear and not circular on plan. They are all in their own way impressive structures, but Castle Sween, crouched on a rocky ridge beside Loch Sween, is arguably the most awesome of all (**colour plate 3**). It is also one of the few that we can date reasonably closely by its architecture, for the quadrangular enclosure has shallow pilaster angle buttresses at the four corners, similar to what we saw at Aberdour (**14**). Such clasping buttresses are indicative of a date around 1200, in which case Sween and Aberdour together are the oldest datable standing castles in Scotland. Confidence in this remarkably early date is further underpinned at Sween by the simple, round-headed entrance gateway through the south wall, similarly contained within a pilaster buttress.

There is nothing quite like Castle Sween anywhere else on the western seaboard, and Castle Tioram, in Loch Moidart, is more truly representative of the group (**15**). It stands proudly on top of a rocky promontory which is cut off from the shore at high tide. The enclosing curtain wall is over 2m (6ft) thick and rises to an average height of 10m (33ft) (but to twice that along the seaward side). A towering height and a massive thickness are characteristics of the curtain-walled stone castles of the thirteenth century. The height gave an immediate advantage to the defenders in this pre-gunpowder age; the thickness not only made life more difficult for the miner but gave sufficient width to support a wall-walk on the battlements.

Bothwell

Postern

Donjon

Entrance

Kildrummy

Donjon

Water Gate

Great Hall

Chapel

Entrance

Site of Postern

Caerlaverock

Entrance

Inverlochy

Entrance

Donjon

Water Gate

Dirleton

Postern

Entrance

Donjon

Rothesay

Postern

Entrance

Sween

Postern

Entrance

Kinclaven

Entrance

Postern

14 Some thirteenth-century curtain-walled castle plans compared.

The curtain wall is almost entirely featureless – there are neither windows nor slits – and only the two entrances (one, the old postern, now blocked) and the embattled parapet relieve the grey severity of the curtain. The tall tower house that rises above the wall in the north-west corner was clearly added at a much later date and there is now no evidence of the form the original residential buildings took. But Tioram retains much of its original defensive arrangements. These include a small stone box-machicolation supported on stone corbels above the main entrance from where one of the defending garrison could 'cover' the vulnerable gateway (there are traces of another over the postern); a stone stair hugging the inside face of the wall giving access to the battlements; and the battlemented wall-head itself, with its wall-walk protected on both sides by parapet walls, and clear signs in the put-log holes on the outer face and the scarcements along the inner face that the wall-walk was originally protected by timber hoards.

Castle Tioram was the principal stronghold of the chief of the Clan MacRuari, descended from Somerled. Other 'sons of Somerled' have left a similar legacy, including the MacDougalls at Dunollie and Dunstaffnage, both close to Oban, and the MacDonalds at Mingary, in Ardnamurchan. Similar castles in the group include Duart on Mull, Duntrune in Loch Creran, and Dunvegan on Skye. The marked

15 Castle Tioram, Loch Moidart, Argyllshire. The lofty, thick curtain wall was largely defended from the battlements, either from the little box machicolation sticking out over the entrance gate (on the right) or from projecting timber hoards (now gone) supported on timbers placed in the putlog holes (visible near the wall-top).

16 An impression of the MacDougalls' residence at Dunstaffnage, beside the Firth of Lorn, Argyllshire, as it might have looked about 1275. The projecting round towers may have been early additions to the original sub-rectangular enclosure wall. Drawn by David Simon.

similarity of these castles begs the question of whether a single hand was involved in their design and execution. Of all these, only Dunstaffnage has round towers projecting from the curtain wall and openings through it, in the form of 'fish-tail' arrow-slits and lancet windows (16). Recent excavations there raise the intriguing possibility that the main north tower was an early addition to the curtain-wall; in which case all three towers, and quite possibly all the openings through the curtain wall also, may not be original.

The arrow-slits and windows at Dunstaffnage are among the few architectural details throughout the entire group which are reasonably closely dated – to some time in the thirteenth century. The owners of Dunstaffnage during this time are also well documented, making this castle an important guide to the rationale behind the building of these alien constructions.

At the time of the Norwegian attack on Rothesay in 1230, Sir Duncan MacDougall, a grandson of Somerled, was lord of Lorn, an extensive maritime lordship; in fact, it was Duncan and his two brothers, Gillespec and Dugald, who led the assault against the Stewarts' Bute stronghold. Contrary to what one might believe, Duncan and his peers were no 'small-time' petty chiefs operating on the very fringe of the known world; they were major landholders, had large forces and fleets at their disposal, and wielded significant political clout. Duncan moved easily between the two realms that competed for his loyalty, and journeyed widely, including to Rome as an ambassador of the king of Scots in 1237. His travelling clearly broadened his mind for in about 1230 he established at Ardchattan, beside Loch Etive, a priory for Valliscaulian monks from Burgundy. In the light of this, his building a formidable castle in the European tradition need come as no surprise.

Duncan's son, Ewen, who inherited the lordship in the 1240s, followed in the same mould. Initially throwing in his lot with King Hakon, he succeeded in becoming 'king' over all the Isles, from Man to Lewis. However, by the time of Hakon's expedition in 1263, Ewen had transferred his allegiance back to the king of Scots, which in the short term led to his imprisonment but which turned out to be a shrewd move in view of what then happened to the Norsemen. Ewen MacDougall of Lorn now became pre-eminent in the region, the Scottish king's chief representative in Kintyre, Argyll and Lorn. We can see this reinforced power and prestige being reflected in a flurry of building activity; it is tempting to ascribe to him the projecting round towers and the great hall along the east side of the enclosure at Dunstaffnage, which together furnished the lord with much improved private and public accommodation.

Hall castles

Formidable enclosures were not the only form of castle introduced into the west at this period. At Aros on Mull, Carrick on Loch Goil, and Skipness in Kintyre are rare examples of hall castles. There were doubtless more, but being less substantial structures they have not survived so well the rigours of time. Recent excavations at the Campbell stronghold of Carrick may provide the first archaeological dating for the construction of these somewhat unusual structures, the architectural dating of which has hitherto ranged across the spectrum from the late thirteenth to the late fourteenth centuries; if the Saintonge ware found in the primary levels relates to the construction of the present impressive structure, then a date in the closing years of the thirteenth century seems the most likely.

Skipness Castle is an example of just how vulnerable these hall castles were to change. The present stronghold looks for all the world like a mighty enclosure castle dating from the close of the thirteenth century, but embedded in the fabric are substantial remains of the earlier hall castle. This comprised two free-standing buildings, one a two-storey residence, with the lord's hall on the upper floor – hence the generic name – and the other a single-storey chapel. There may well have been other structures as well, and everything would probably have been enclosed within a defensive wall of earth and timber (17). Skipness was held by the MacSweens in the middle of the century, and it is possible that this more modest castle was a subsidiary residence to their main house beside Loch Sween.

All these strongholds, whether curtain-walled castles or hall castles, were built primarily as residences for their lords but there is clear evidence that they were built very much with royal approval, and with the distinct possibility that the monarchs themselves might desire to use them on those occasions when they were in the region. Alexander III's charter to Gilchrist MacNachtan, lord of Fraoch Eilean Castle in

17 An impression of how Skipness Castle, on the east coast of Kintyre, Argyllshire, might have looked originally, before its conversion into a mighty curtain-walled castle about 1300. Drawn by David Simon.

Loch Awe, empowers him 'to have the custody of our castle and island of Frechelan, so that they may cause the said castle to be built at our expense, and to repair it whenever necessary, and to keep it in safety for our needs, and to make the said castle, honourably prepared, open for us to dwell in on such occasions when we may come there'.

These castles of the western seaboard are quite extraordinary strongholds. Here in Argyll and the Isles, far beyond the Norman pale, rose some of the most impressive castles built in the thirteenth century to rival anything being constructed in the realm of Scotland itself. Yet Suibhne (Sven) 'the Red', the builder of Castle Sween, and his peers were not feudal aristocrats

of Norman stock but chiefs with mixed Norse-Celtic roots. What possessed them to build as they did will forever remain a mystery, but our legacy of castles is the greater for their efforts.

Mainland castles of the great and grand

The winning of the west for Scotland was achieved in large part through the endeavours of the Stewarts. It was Walter, first of the hereditary Stewarts, who very probably defeated and killed Somerled himself in battle near Renfrew in 1164; and it was his son, Alan, who made the first inroads into the western sea when he took control of the Island of Bute some time before 1200. Sixty years later, Walter Stewart, earl of Menteith (see 23), contrived to oust Dugald MacSween, son of Sween 'the Red', from the lordship of Knapdale.

The Stewarts, unlike the MacSweens, were fully paid-up members of the Anglo-Norman aristocracy and the building of high and mighty stone castles, to replace their more modest timber strongholds of the previous century, would for them have been the perfectly natural thing to do. In this they were mirroring the activities of their close relatives in England, in particular the FitzAlan lords of Oswestry, the descendants of Walter (I)'s eldest brother, who during the course of the twelfth century built impressive masonry castles at Arundel (Sussex) and Clun (Shropshire) on top of or, in the case of Clun, into the original earthworks. Given the close family ties binding the Stewarts despite their residing in different countries, and given also the fact that the Scottish Stewarts retained certain English estates inherited from Walter (I), we can picture Walter's descendants becoming familiar with these and other English castles as they travelled south to visit relatives and friends and administer their lands. In this the Stewarts were far from alone, and we should never underestimate the amount of travelling undertaken by the Scottish aristocracy in those

far-off days, and particularly the extent of their contacts with their English peers.

Nothing survives above ground of Renfrew Castle, the Stewarts' chief residence, which is a great pity for it must have been something to marvel at if what we have left at their two other principal seats, Dundonald and Rothesay, is anything to go by. Dundonald has only recently been excavated to reveal more of the sophisticated castle built on that prominent hill-top towards the close of the century. Rothesay on the other hand stands remarkably intact (18), albeit somewhat altered down the centuries, and although its original date of construction is not possible to determine it was most probably built

18 Rothesay Castle, the Stewart stronghold on Bute. The original circular curtain wall, built about 1200, was furnished with projecting round towers, a battered wall base and crenellations in the later thirteenth century. The imposing gatehouse on the left was added by King James IV about 1500.

either by Alan, who died in 1204, or his son, Walter (II). Rothesay and Castle Sween are thus contemporary.

Despite the obvious difference in their shapes – Rothesay being circular (see **14**) and Sween rectangular – the two castles in their original states were much alike. Rothesay shared the same solidly thick stone curtain wall – a well-nigh impregnable shell (though they reckoned without the Norsemen and their axes!) within which were placed the main castle buildings, now all gone. The main entrance was a single timber door set behind plain stone jambs terminating at the top in a round arch and secured by a draw-bar; the postern was similar. There were no other openings through the curtain wall, except perhaps for the crenellations at the wall-head, reached from the courtyard by two straightish flights of stairs. (The crenellations visible today date from the modifications carried out later in the century and we shall return to these on pages 41–2).

The strong curtain wall with the emphasis on wall-head defence was the chief characteristic of the great thirteenth-century castle. Typical is Kinclaven Castle, close to the confluence of the rivers Isla and Tay north of Perth. It survives only as an ivy-clad ruin and has never been excavated, but we know that it was built by the crown between 1210 and 1236 following the destruction in a great flood of the royal castle at Perth. The square curtain wall encloses a substantial area 40m (131ft) across which would once have been crammed with buildings (see **14**). A modest amount of accommodation would also have been provided in the small towers projecting from the curtain, one at each corner, and although little remains of these they may have been similar to the latrine tower projecting from one of Sween's corners. Similar rectangular towers projected out from the curtain wall at another imposing early thirteenth-century castle, Balvenie, near Dufftown in Glenfiddich (Banffshire), built most probably by William Comyn, earl of Buchan, who died in 1233. Also visible at Balvenie, but

gone from Kinclaven, is a stretch of wall-walk on the battlements of the curtain. Gone from Balvenie but existing at Kinclaven is the straight stone stair giving access to the wall-head.

Two significant developments affected these simple curtain-walled castles as the century progressed. One was the addition of large round towers to the angles of the curtain, and the other was the strengthening of the entrance defences. Both seem to have been prompted chiefly by a need to upgrade security, but the towers also contributed to improvements in the accommodation.

Projecting round towers first made their appearance in castles around 1200; Chateau-Gaillard, the extraordinary castle overlooking the River Seine, in northern France, may well have been a major influence in their gradual spread in the early years of the century. The earliest instance in Scotland that can be dated with a degree of confidence to the second quarter of the century is Dirleton Castle, in East Lothian, built by John de Vaux (**19** and see **14**). Though the de Vauxs had close family links with England – John's cousin, Robert, was lord of Gilsland in Cumbria – it seems more likely that the inspiration for the multi-towered Dirleton Castle was drawn from France. John de Vaux became steward to Marie de Coucy following her marriage to King Alexander II in 1239. Marie was the daughter of Duke Enguerrand (III), lord of Coucy in northern France. Enguerrand's castle, built in the 1220s, was destroyed by German soldiers during the First World War but we are fortunate in that MacGibbon and Ross recorded it a generation earlier. They showed it to be a mighty polygonal curtain-walled enclosure with four formidable round towers projecting from the angles and a massive round tower, or donjon, dominating all. John de Vaux must surely have visited Coucy while accompanying his queen on her visits home; he can have been nothing but overwhelmed by what he saw.

John de Vaux's motive for building such a formidable residence must surely have been his

19 Dirleton Castle, East Lothian. The cluster of projecting round and rectangular towers in the foreground provided private accommodation for Lord and Lady de Vaux.

earnest desire to display wealth and status. He was after all no marcher lord but a landed nobleman holding a comparatively small but exceptionally rich barony in the heart of the kingdom – a kingdom largely at peace with itself, and with its southern neighbour thanks to the Treaty of York signed in 1237. The only conflict of any substance was taking place in the Norse dominions many miles to the west. Herein lies one of the contradictions of the medieval castle. It originated in the tenth and eleventh centuries in times of strife to help protect and defend, but such times were not conducive to the building of large, imposing and costly residences. For Lord de Vaux to be in a position to build a great stone castle he needed to have three things: he had to have the wealth to build it; he had to have reliable tenure of his lands; and he had to have lengthy periods of

peace to carry out the building works, which would have taken several seasons to complete.

The Stewart who built Rothesay was operating in a frontier zone and probably had a different agenda, motivated more by the needs of defence than residence. This same sense of urgency seems also to have prompted the remodelling of the castle during the century, possibly in the aftermath of the Norse attack of 1230, perhaps as a result of the momentous events in the 1260s. The measures taken to upgrade the defences included the strengthening of the main entrance with a portcullis, alterations to the wall-head crenellations, and the building of four round towers out from the curtain wall. In heightening the curtain wall in the sixteenth-century the masons built upon these earlier defences and so preserved them. They are a very precious survival. They comprised broad upstanding merlons interspersed by narrower crenelles through which the archers standing on the wall-walk behind would have fired off their weapons (**20**).

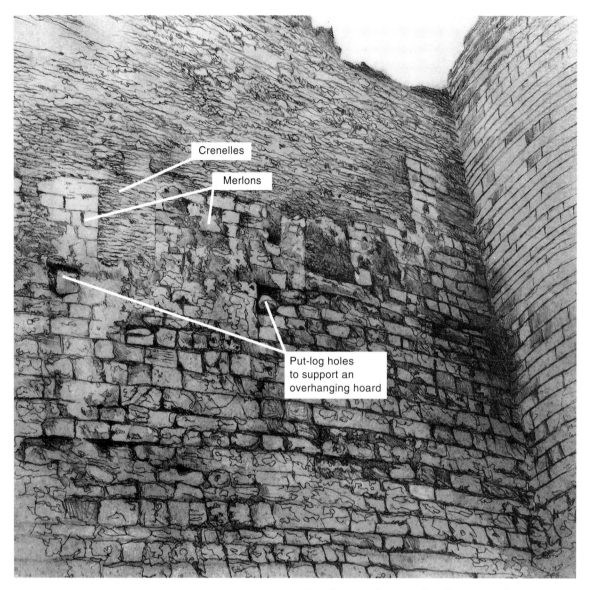

Crenelles

Merlons

Put-log holes
to support an
overhanging hoard

20 The crenellations at Rothesay Castle, Bute, grafted onto the original wallhead of the curtain in the later thirteenth century. Drawn by David Simon.

The crenellations were stepped up to meet the wall-tops of the towers themselves. These towers, three storeys high, had splayed (or battered) bases with the intention that missiles dropped from the battlements would ricochet out into the faces of the enemy attempting to mine the walls. The only openings were tall, slender arrow-slits with shovel-shaped enlargements at top and bottom.

Caerlaverock – a tale of two castles

The development of the curtain-walled castle from the relatively simple rectangular form to the more complex round-towered type is well illustrated at Caerlaverock, situated at the mouth of the Nith estuary in Dumfriesshire. Caerlaverock has not one but two castles and, as luck would have it, the construction date for both was accurately established in the 1970s by dendrochronology. The older castle, 'the one in the woods', was shown to have been built in the mid-1220s, coinciding with the granting of the barony to Sir John de Maccuswell, or Maxwell,

21 Caerlaverock Castle, near Glencaple, Dumfriesshire. Although much of the upstanding masonry belongs to the fourteenth century and later, the unique triangular plan dates from the time of the castle's foundation in the 1270s.

who chose to transfer his chief seat from his ancestral estate near Roxburgh Castle in the eastern Borders (see 32) to his new lordship. This site was 'excavated' in the 1860s and found to be quadrangular in plan with small rectangular towers projecting from the curtain at several points, in the manner of Kinclaven.

The Caerlaverock Castle that so impresses visitors today was built 200m (218 yards) to the north of the original castle about 1277, the date the drawbridge timbers were felled (21 and 22). The Maxwell lord at this date was Herbert, Sir John's nephew, but his reasons for going to such time, trouble and expense after barely fifty years can only be guessed at; the most convincing explanation is that the first castle had been built too near the salt-marsh of the Solway Firth and had become unstable. The 'mark 2' castle was quite different from its predecessor. The writer of the splendid poem, the *Roll of Karlaverock*, composed in celebration of King Edward of England's great attack on the castle in 1300, described it perfectly: 'In shape it was like a shield, for it had but three sides round it, with a tower at each corner, but one of them was a double one, so high, so long, and so wide, that the gate was underneath it, well made and strong, with a drawbridge and a sufficiency of other defences' (see 14).

Other members of the 'great and grand' were moved to build in a manner similar to Herbert de Maxwell, and examples may be seen throughout the country. Caerlaverock was unique in being triangular; the others were more conventionally shaped. Even here there was variety, particularly regarding the location of the principal lordly accommodation. Some had, like Caerlaverock, the twin-towered gatehouse serving as the keep, and these have been christened 'keep-gatehouses'. The royal castle at Kirkcudbright seems to have been of this form, and the Stewart stronghold at Dundonald also. In fact, recent excavation has shown that Dundonald had two imposing gatehouses, similar to the Edwardian castles at Rhuddlan

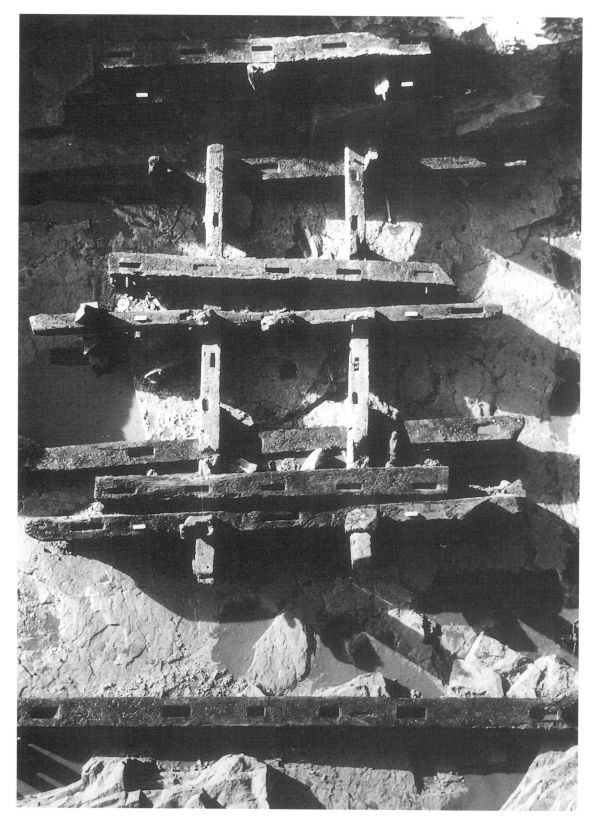

22 The drawbridge timbers discovered in 1962 during excavation of the inner moat at Caerlaverock Castle. The building of the original bridge was ascribed by dendrochronology to the 1270s, a subsequent repair to the 1330s, and a complete replacement to the 1370s, dates which mirror the fortunes of Scotland before, during and after the wars with England.

and Beaumaris in Wales. One gatehouse faced eastward into Scotland and the other westward to the Firth of Clyde and the Stewarts' newly acquired island dominions.

The majority of castles, however, had the lord's residence housed in a mighty tower, or donjon (the word has subsequently been corrupted into 'dungeon', with an altogether different meaning), placed elsewhere along the curtain wall's circuit. John Comyn's formidable stronghold at Inverlochy in Lochaber (Inverness-shire) is the perfect illustration of this. There the rectangular curtain wall has four round towers, one at each corner (see **14**). Three are identical but that at the north-west corner is 3m (10ft) bigger in girth. The castle built by the earl of Mar at Kildrummy in Strathdon (Aberdeenshire) has a polygonal-shaped curtain wall with several round towers projecting from it, but that at the west corner, the Snow Tower, is over 4m (13ft) larger than the Warden Tower at the north corner (see **14**). Kildrummy also has a twin-towered gatehouse, sadly now surviving as foundation walls only, but there is good reason for thinking that this element was grafted onto the curtain wall during the English occupation of the early 1300s.

There is no getting away from the fact that each castle was different from the next, despite the common use of the basic ingredients – high curtain wall and projecting round towers. Various arguments have been advanced as to why, for example, some castles had the lord's residence over the gatehouse and others had it housed in a donjon at the rear of the enclosure. As far as I am aware no one has advanced the possibility that the difference was the result of personal preference, of 'one man's meat being

another man's poison'. Many things may have changed down the intervening centuries, but one thing is for sure, human nature has not; and man's penchant for doing the unpredictable was probably just as true then as it is today.

The baronial household

To understand better how the baronial castle functioned as a residence we have to know something of the structure of a great nobleman's household. Unfortunately there are few surviving documents which give us an insight into the workings of a Scottish baronial family, and we have to complement what we have with those relating to baronial families in England. This seems reasonable enough, for several Scottish noble families held estates south of the Border, but we must exercise caution when doing so; in 1295 the annual income of the earl of Fife was assessed at £500 thus placing the leading earl of the Scottish realm on a financial par with a modest English baron. The exercise, however, is worthwhile for it enables us to peep into their world, a world so different from our own.

The baronial household would have been varied in composition and its members considerable in number. In fact, there would probably have been more than one household, for the lady of the castle would have had a household, and an independence, of her own. Lord and lady would have lived largely separate lives, he forever travelling about, visiting his various estates, attending on his king and so forth, she residing more permanently at the castle, seeing to the running of the place and the upbringing of the family (**23**). The children in their early years would have stayed in the castle, though they were largely brought up by nurses who were expected to feed, wash, teach and comfort them. It was usual for children from about the age of five, girls as well as boys, to be sent away to another noble household to further their education. They would return in their early teens to take their place in the bosom of the family once more. Girls were normally married by the age of 14, whereas boys generally waited

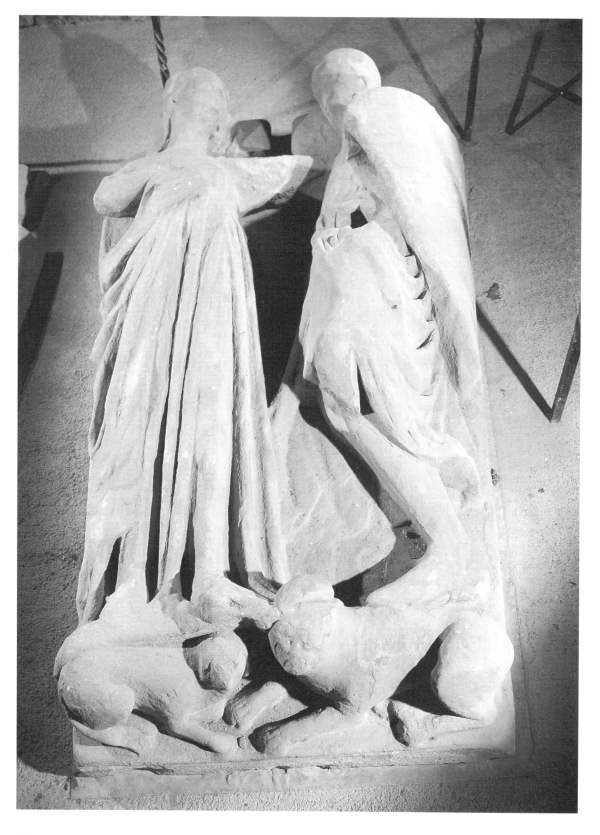

23 The Countess Mary of Menteith clasps her lord, Walter Stewart, affectionately to her bosom on their double effigy, now on display in the chapter house at Inchmahome Priory, in the Lake of Menteith, Stirlingshire. The loving couple, who together accompanied the maid Margaret, daughter of King Alexander III, to Norway in 1282 for her marriage to King Eric II, were buried side by side in the choir of the priory church.

until they had come of age and into possession of land in their own right.

Life in the castle was male-dominated; women had a very low profile. Other than her ladyship herself, her ladies-in-waiting, the nurses and perhaps the laundress, almost everyone else was male, though oddly enough the beer was often produced by an ale-wife! Given the large numbers in the household and the cramped nature of the accommodation, perhaps this largely all-male world was just as well. The household comprised men from all levels of society. There was the body of knights, squires and men-at-arms who provided the lord with his quota of military service (**24**); the small nucleus of senior officials who managed his affairs; the larger group of lesser office-bearers who carried through the wide range of functions required to sustain the lifestyle of a great nobleman; and the vast underbelly of 'gofers'. All told there may have been as many as 150 people living and working in and around a great castle.

At the top of the tree was the steward. It was his duty to supervise the managing of the estates and the running of the household. There might in fact have been two stewards, for by the mid-thirteenth century it was becoming common practice to separate out estate management from household management. The estate steward would have been a man of noble birth in his own right, not far removed in rank from the lord himself and very probably residing on his own manor, where he too would have been served by his own more modest household. The household steward on the other hand is more likely to have been of less noble birth and to have lived more permanently at his lord's castle

in his own quarters. To him fell the task of ensuring the smooth running of a busy and varied complex that was expected to function as family home, soldiers' barracks, guest-house, estate office, law court and prison.

In this the steward would have been assisted by other officials. These would have included the constable, responsible for security, the chamberlain or treasurer, in charge of the finances, and the pantler and butler, who together looked after the provision of food and

24 The effigy of an armed knight of the Stewart earls of Menteith, on display in the chapter house at Inchmahome Priory.

drink. The spiritual side of things was administered by the chaplain, and the almoner salved the lord's conscience by attending to the poor at the gate. Beyond the immediate confines of the courtyard was the marshal, who had charge of the many horses and the baggage-train which transported the lord and lady and their travelling household around the country.

Each official had charge of a host of assistants, lower-ranking servants and menials who actually carried out the work. Under the constable were the porters, who guarded the castle gates, and the door-wards or ushers, who watched the doors leading into the great hall and the private apartments of the lord and lady. The chaplain was served by several clerks, including the clerk of the offices and the clerk of the chapel. In the kitchens, working to the direction of the pantler and butler, was a proliferation of cooks, larderers, saucers, pantrymen, bakers, brewsters and poulterers. Elsewhere there was the tailor, the barber-surgeon who let blood and drew teeth as well as shaved his betters, and the chandler who ensured that folk didn't fall down the winding stairs. Beyond the courtyard, under the watchful eye of the marshal, were the sumpters, farriers, grooms, carters and messengers who went hither and yon about the realm with dispatches. Of course, not every baronial household would have been so extensive; everything was relative. But somebody of the highest rank and station, like Walter of Moray, lord of Bothwell, might well have commanded something approaching the complement given above.

Bothwell and the castle as residence

Bothwell, built beside a winding in the River Clyde 12km (7½ miles) south-east of the centre of Glasgow, is without any doubt the most imposing of all the great thirteenth-century castles, then as today (**colour plate 4**; see also **54**). Not for nothing has it been called 'the grandest piece of secular architecture that the Middle Ages have bequeathed to us in Scotland'. In common with its contemporaries, Bothwell has suffered down the centuries, but despite the

various prolonged and bloody medieval sieges and the undermining by colliers of more recent times, the walls still stand today, monumentally impressive. It is the perfect castle to illustrate how life was lived in these mighty fortress-residences. And there was no one greater or grander than Walter of Moray, who acquired the lordship of Bothwell in 1242 on the death of his father-in-law, Walter Olifard II, and who very probably began the building of the mighty castle. In fact, so grand were the Morays that Walter's son and heir, William, who succeeded him in 1278, was known as 'the Rich'.

With the picture of a great baronial household in our minds, the enormous scale of Bothwell Castle begins to make sense (see **14**). It matters not one jot that the original scheme for a huge polygonal-shaped courtyard covering 0.75 hectares (1.8 acres) (putting it on a par with mighty Caernarfon) never reached fruition – perhaps William 'the Rich' became 'the Poor' as his money ran out, or maybe the wars with England after 1296 intervened – for it does not in any way detract from the intended magnitude of his castle or deflect from our appreciation of the enormous size of his household. If in our mind's eye we people the now quiet and ghostly ruined castle with a great household such as I have described, we can perhaps begin to imagine what life in a great thirteenth-century castle would have been like (**25**). Just imagine the stench from the cess-pits at the bases of the latrine chutes! No wonder they chose to move about from place to place at frequent intervals, giving a chance for the steward to arrange for a good clean out.

Bothwell's mighty curtain had five round towers projecting from it. One of them was a twin-towered gatehouse which would most likely have provided quite commodious living

25 An impression of how the mighty castle of the Morays at Bothwell, beside the River Clyde in Lanarkshire, might have looked in 1275 had the original building programme been completed. On the far bank of the Clyde is Blantyre Priory, a small Augustinian house founded around the 1240s by the earl of Dunbar. Drawn by David Simon.

26 The mighty donjon at Bothwell, the Morays' private residence in the castle.

quarters in its upper floors for the constable and his personal servants. Three of the other four towers would also have provided apartments for other senior officials on their upper floors, each perhaps comprising two rooms – a hall on the first floor and a private chamber containing the bed on the second, directly beneath the battlements. The rooms would have had fireplaces and latrines *en suite*. The personal servants might have slept on shake-downs laid out either on the floor of the bed-chamber or in the passage outside the door.

The ground floors of all the towers were given over to stores, whether for arms and ammunition, for food and drink, or for other miscellaneous items. The smallest of the three towers 'stored' prisoners in both its ground floor and basement. Imprisonment was not a form of punishment in the Middle Ages, not formally anyway, though it seems that many an unfortunate was thrown into prison and suitably forgotten about. Poor Sir Patrick Lindsay, for example, was cast into a dark dungeon in Rothesay Castle in 1489 and told to 'sitt quhair he should not sie his feet for ane year'. Prisons like that at Bothwell were more commonly used to hold suspected criminals until they could be brought for trial in the baron court where, if they were found guilty, they would be sentenced to other forms of punishment, like paying a fine or losing a hand. The two-tier prison at Bothwell – the prison and pit – is a good example of many a castle prison in Scotland. The upper level is reasonably well-ventilated and lit by the narrow arrow-slits and with an *en suite* latrine; the miserable pit beneath lacks sanitation, light or air. We assume that the prison itself was for the freemen in society and the pit for the serf class. Those of noble birth would normally have been held under permanent guard in one of the officials' apartments.

The largest of the towers, the mighty donjon, was the residence of the lord and his immediate family (**26**). Even today in its ruined state it impresses, just as it was intended to overawe those who gazed on it all those years ago. Everything about it proclaims that therein resided a man of immense power and wealth. The red sandstone masonry is of the highest quality ashlars, the architectural detail is restrained but refined, and the planning is so carefully and cunningly thought out that it provided both a spacious and a secure suite of rooms. The accommodation was spread over four floors: a storage basement complete with well, a ground-floor reception hall, and two upper floors which probably formed the lordly apartment itself.

Despite the fact that one half of 'that stalwart toure' has now gone, cast down in 1337 by its owner, Sir Andrew Moray, in order to prevent the castle from being garrisoned again by the English, the remainder stands largely complete from basement to wall-head. The huge courtyard on the other hand is now devoid of its clutter of buildings. Pride of place would have been the hall block, probably a two-storey timber structure, located for the lord's convenience near the donjon. The great hall itself on the upper floor would have been the setting for all the great occasions – large feasts, gatherings of the household and tenantry, sittings of the baron court. Below it, at ground level, may have been a 'laigh' or lower hall, or perhaps storage space. The kitchens, bakehouses and stores would have stood close by. Elsewhere there would have been the brewhouse, stables, workshops, even perhaps a little castle garden for the lord and lady's use and a kitchen garden growing vegetables and herbs. Beyond the curtain and enclosing outer ditch would have been orchards, dovecots, rabbit warrens and the fields and forests which provided the wherewithal to keep this enormous household going.

Lesser castles

The castles referred to above were without exception the chief residences of the elite in society, the royal family and the leading magnates. But below them were castles of lesser magnitude. These served a variety of functions. Some were subsidiary residences of the great and grand, perhaps located on an outlying estate, serving as a hunting-lodge or possibly protecting a feature of strategic importance like a harbour or river crossing. Others were the permanent residences of the lesser nobility. These might be knights holding their lands as sub-tenancies of the main fief; they might be noblemen serving as high-ranking officials in a mighty lord's retinue, like that of estate steward; or they might be barons of second rank holding their lands as individual fiefs directly of the crown. As might be expected, these lesser castles were less impressive structures than the likes of Bothwell. Most of them were the timber castles constructed in the previous century, while those built during the course of the thirteenth century continued to use the readily available raw materials of earth, clay and wood in preference to the more costly stone and lime. There were, however, notable exceptions.

Rattray – a secondary residence

We have already encountered the little castle at Rattray on the Buchan coast north of Aberdeen (page 25). Built in the twelfth century, the motte seems to have been abandoned for a short while in the early years of the thirteenth century before once again being put to good use. The date of reoccupation coincides with the acquisition about 1211 of the earldom of Buchan by William Comyn. The Comyns established their chief seat, the formidable stone stronghold at Balvenie, in Glen Fiddich, 80km (50 miles) inland from Rattray. Rattray Castle can only have been a subsidiary stronghold from where Comyn's constable could control the small port and town that had grown up beside the Loch of Strathbeg, then a sea-loch. If the Comyns visited at all it would have been only very occasionally. The more likely scenario would be the constable making his way across country to Balvenie to report to his master. The excavations on top of the motte hill at Rattray revealed a well-built aisled hall, probably of timber construction, as well as some ovens; altogether a quite different scale of living to that no doubt witnessed at Balvenie.

Strachan – a hunting-lodge

Hunting was an important leisure pursuit of the medieval nobility and most great castles would have had forests or deer parks associated with them. Considerable time would be spent away from the main residence by the great and grand looking for sport, and so hunting-lodges were common. These were generally defensive in form, like Alexander II's hunting-castle at Clunie, in the southern foothills of the Grampians, or Alan Durward's spacious motte, the Peel of Lumphanan, built within 4km (2½ miles) of his chief residence, Coull Castle, about 1250, and close to the spot where King Macbeth was actually killed in 1057.

Castlehill of Strachan, a low, flat-topped mound protruding from the floodplain of the River Feugh in Royal Deeside (Aberdeenshire), is a good example that has been recently excavated. William Giffard, whose chief seat was at Yester Castle, near Gifford (East Lothian), had been granted the barony of Strachan by King William I about 1195. The charter recording the gift stipulated that the estate was to be held 'in forest'. The excavations carried out there in 1980–1 showed that the motte was not actually built until about 1250, and it may be that the original hunt-hall was a less formidable structure. The summit of the motte was largely taken up by a circular timber building, presumably providing the main accommodation and partitioned internally; it may or may not have been two-storeyed (**27**). Intriguingly, outside the building and within the courtyard enclosed by the timber palisade were several oven bases formed from millstones. It is tempting to see these as medieval barbecues, around which the hunting-party gathered at the end of a hard day's sport, eating and drinking their fill and regaling each other with tales that were as long as the night.

Muirhouselaw – a moated manor

The permanent residences of those on the next rungs down the social ladder, the knights and the lairds, seem generally to have taken a similar form to the lesser castles of the elite in society. Mottes, ringworks, island fastnesses and crannogs constructed by forebears in the preceding century continued to be occupied.

However, a new form of fortified home – the moated homestead or manor – probably made its appearance in Scotland during the century, although there has been an almost complete absence of excavation to verify this. It seems reasonable to assume that the development mirrored that south of the Border where much more work has been done. The picture emerging there is of moated sites originating in the latter half of the twelfth century and proliferating during the course of the next two centuries.

Moated sites come in all shapes and sizes. Hallyards (Perthshire), known only from aerial photographs, measures 85 by 80m (279 by 262ft), whereas that at nearby Links is a mere 30m (98ft) square. The laird of Hallyards is not known but, if size is anything to go by, he must have been higher up the social ladder than the probable builder of Links, William, son of Alexander, a tenant of Richard de Montfiquet, lord of the barony of Cargill, where there is a fine ringwork. Moats could be quite complex in form. The site at Gelston (Kirkcudbrightshire), now also largely visible only from the air, has two adjacent moated enclosures, one perhaps serving as an outer court to the main residence, in much the same way as the bailey served the motte (**colour plate 5**). That at nearby Dunrod was demonstrably an integral part of a developed community, with a church and village close by.

Muirhouselaw Moat (Roxburghshire) is a fine example. It comprises two contiguous enclosures of unequal size, the larger measuring 70sq m (753sq ft), the smaller about half that size. Both were surrounded by a broad, flat-bottomed ditch evidently intended to be filled with water. Within the larger enclosure are the

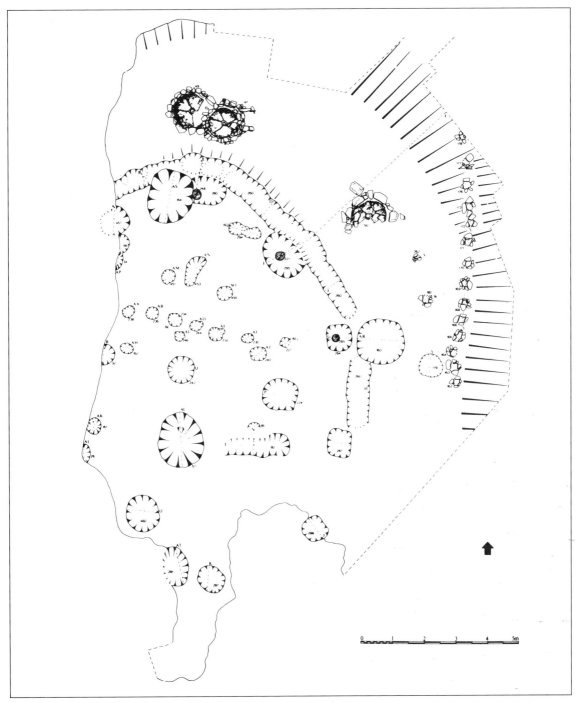

27 Plan of the features discovered on top of the Castlehill of Strachan, Aberdeenshire.

stone foundations of two structures, the larger one a two-roomed building measuring about 20 by 9m (66 by 30ft) and the smaller one 5sq m (54sq ft). We can postulate that the former was the hall block for more public activities, and the latter a square tower housing the lord's private

Stirling itself endured a particularly bitter siege in the late spring and early summer of 1304. By then it was clear to Edward of England that his subjugation of Scotland would not be achieved until he retook Stirling. During the winter of 1303 Edward, safe within his headquarters at Dunfermline Abbey, finalized his siege plan. He would take no chances; a formidable array of siege engines, seventeen at least, was to be deployed. So proud were the English of their artillery that they had pet names for them. One was called 'Bothwell', presumably 'le berefrey' that had been at the siege of Bothwell three year earlier. Another had the terrifying name of 'war wolf'. Quite what 'war wolf' did is not made clear, but it may have been a trebuchet, a mighty stone-throwing machine, for when it was fired at the castle it devastated

30 Scottish artillery at the siege of Carlisle, 1315, from Edward II's charter to the English Border city, granted in the following year.

the gatehouse. In truth, the English king had no need to deploy 'war wolf' at all for the garrison had previously surrendered, so depriving Edward of the thrill of seeing his latest 'toy' in action for the first time. Not to be denied his moment of pleasure, he ungraciously ordered part of the Scots' garrison back into the castle so that he might show off his new weapon.

War engines clearly played an important role in siege warfare, as the illustration appearing on the charter granted in 1316 to the city of Carlisle for resisting the Scots in the previous year so tellingly shows (30), but they were only part of the story. The twenty miners at the siege of

Bothwell were there presumably to attempt to cut their way either through or under the castle walls, much like the Norse had done at Rothesay in 1230, their purpose being to cause a collapse so that the awaiting infantry might rush through the breach and take on the defenders in hand-to-hand fighting. These aggressive acts were supported by more passive tactics, the 'waiting game' by which the castle was blockaded and the defenders prevented from gaining fresh supplies. Many a siege was allowed to drag on in the knowledge that eventually those within the castle would be reduced to starvation, as Stephen de Brampton experienced at Bothwell. For this reason, garrisons, knowing they were about to be besieged, took the precaution of stocking up in advance. Unfortunately, this worked against the unlucky garrison defending Kildrummy in the summer of 1306; they were compelled to surrender to the English when the fire that began in the great hall, where extra grain had temporarily been stored, quickly got out of control and spread throughout the castle.

The siege of Caerlaverock, 1300

The progress of the majority of the sieges may only be glimpsed at in contemporary records, mainly financial accounts and monastic annals. But there was one siege, the English investment of Caerlaverock Castle in July 1300, for which we have full details (**colour plate 6**). The *Roll of Karlaverock*, a snippet from which introduced this chapter, is a remarkable poem for it gives us a blow-by-blow account, literally, of the action by someone who actually witnessed it. The author was an unnamed herald serving in Edward of England's army as it set out from Carlisle on 1 July to invade Galloway. No matter that the poet's prime purpose in penning it was to record the heraldry of the English knights-in-arms, nor that his language is dripping with hyperbole for dramatic effect; it nevertheless remains a wonderful word-picture of the whole process of besieging a castle.

The English force that arrived before Caerlaverock on that day in July numbered 87 knights and 3,000 infantry. The castle garrison ranged against them, we subsequently discover, comprised just sixty men and the lady of the castle, Lady Maxwell; her husband was by then languishing in an English prison. Our poet, though, was under no illusion as to the enormity of the task confronting his side:

Caerlaverock was a castle
So strong, that it did not fear siege,
Before the king came there;

He offered his opinion:

It will not be taken by check with a rook,
But there will be projectiles thrown,
And engines raised and poised.

The besiegers first pitched camp, under the direction of the marshals:

There was many a cord stretched,
Many a peg driven into the ground,

after which they helped the navy to unload the engines and provisions that had newly arrived by sea. The siege could now begin in earnest. The first assault was made by the infantry, who took the full brunt of the garrison's opening salvo:

And might be seen fly among them
Stones, arrows, and quarrels [cross-bow bolts].

The men-at-arms rushed forward in support, but they too came under heavy fire from the defenders stationed at the battlements:

Stones fall so thickly,
As if they would rain them,
And hats and helmets crushed,
Shields and targets broken in pieces;

Defiantly they returned fire, picking up the fallen stones and hurling them back at the defenders, thereby contriving to reach the brink of the ditch. There, one of their number, Thomas de Richmond, stepped boldly forward onto the bridge and shouted out to the defenders demanding entry. The response was predictable, and the stones rained down once more. But still they pressed the attack, with

Adam de la Forde mining at the walls and Richard de Kirkbride assailing the castle gate:

> For never did smith with hammer
> Strike his iron so hard
> As he and his did there.

All to no avail. The huge stones that were showered down on them, along with the arrows and quarrels, eventually forced them to retire. Further waves of attack were likewise repulsed:

> Those within, who are fully expecting it,
> And bend their bows and cross-bows,
> And shoot with their springalds [a mechanical cross-bow],
> And keep themselves equally ready
> Both to throw and to hurl.

Throughout all this, Brother Robert (a holy man of God!) kept up a constant barrage from his stone-firing 'robinet'. But realizing this to be inadequate, he ordered his men to build three much larger engines. The resultant effect was devastating, as the quotation at the beginning of this chapter details. First, the bretasche, or timber hoard protecting the wall-walk, was hit, and one of the defenders sheltering behind it killed. Then the roof behind collapsed under the weight of the hurled stones. The defenders now

had no option but to surrender, and so, after little more than a day of stout resistance:

> The companions begged for peace,
> And put out a pennon.

The author of the *Roll of Karlaverock* leaves us with the firm impression that much of the defence was carried out from the wall-head. This involved men armed not only with longbows and crossbows but also with stones, and very probably anything else that came to hand. Many a castle still has its share of crude sandstone balls lying around, none more so than Caerlaverock itself, while excavation at others has produced plenty of arrowheads and crossbow bolts. A good cross-range was retrieved from Urquhart Castle (Inverness-shire) during clearance work in the 1920s, including a lump of corroded arrowheads, evidently once stored in a bag long since rotted away (**31**).

The archers on the battlements were assisted by others firing small mechanical engines – springalds, firing much larger crossbow bolts,

31 An encrusted mass of iron arrowheads (left) and other weaponry found at Urquhart Castle, Loch Ness, Inverness-shire, in the 1920s. The stone cannonballs (top) were for use by the gunpowder artillery of a later age.

and stone-throwing catapults. Elsewhere in the castle others would be attempting to beat off the assaults. Some would be stationed within the projecting towers firing their arrows and bolts through the narrow slits at the miners hacking at the bases of the walls or at those attempting to batter down the castle gate. The experiences gained and the lessons learned during the course of these 'wars of independence' would lead to improvements being made to castle design. Wall-heads, gateways and outer defences in particular were prime features for recrafting.

English strongholds on Scottish soil

The prolonged attempt by the English to impose themselves on the Scots resulted not only in them using Scottish castles as bases from which to operate but also in them building new strongholds. Unfortunately, despite there being considerable documentary evidence in the English accounts for the repair and rebuilding of captured Scottish castles, little physical evidence survives on the ground. There are just two significant survivals, in addition to the fragments of masonry lurking behind the ivy

atop the mighty castle hill of Roxburgh (**32**). One is at Kildrummy in the north of the country and belongs to the heady days of the first 'war of Independence'; the other is Lochmaben (Dumfriesshire) near the Border and dates to the twilight of the English occupation in the 1360s.

The ruined gatehouse at Kildrummy is so similar to that at Harlech Castle, in north Wales, that its construction has been attributed to King Edward's mason-architect, Master James of St George, who was responsible for building Harlech in the 1280s. Edward twice stayed at Kildrummy, in 1296 and 1303. Shortly after his latter departure, Master James received £100 for work undertaken. The records are not

32 Roxburgh Castle (centre left foreground), strategically positioned between the rivers Tweed (left) and Teviot (right). The fragments of masonry on the summit of the mighty castle hill are a legacy of the lengthy English occupation. The remains of the town of Roxburgh, which at one time was second only to Berwick-upon-Tweed in importance but withered as the English presence continued, lie beneath the green sward beyond the castle. The last siege of Roxburgh Castle in 1460 finally ended the English occupation.

specific, and the work for which he was reimbursed may not even have been carried out at Kildrummy, but the timing and the similarity with Harlech suggest otherwise. The sum involved was large for those days and compares with the £125 paid by Edward for the building of another great north-Welsh castle gatehouse, Conwy.

Master James was one of a number of skilled contractors, if we may call them that, brought to Scotland from Wales after 1296. They included Master Walter of Hereford, master mason at Caernarfon, and Thomas de Houghton, a master carpenter fresh from Beaumaris. Not only were they engaged in repairing and rebuilding captured castles, they were also practically involved in the sieges themselves, constructing siege works and engines. However, their most important contributions have now all but vanished – the stronghold built by Master James at Linlithgow (where King Edward wintered during 1301–2) and other strongholds at Lochmaben and Selkirk. These new works are known as 'peels', from the old French word *pel* meaning stake, for they were built almost entirely of earth and wood.

The peel at Linlithgow (West Lothian) was built around the royal manor-house erected during King David's reign in the twelfth century, where the palace of the later Stewarts now stands. The main element was a great ditch cutting the promontory off from the town to its south, behind which was the peel or palisade, made of split tree trunks. In the centre of the palisade was a strong gatehouse, which possibly incorporated some stonework, and at either end, beside the loch, were wooden towers. A lesser ditch and a palisade were constructed around the remainder of the promontory to defend it from attack from the loch. Inside the peel fresh garrison buildings were erected to complement the old manor-house.

Despite being built largely of earth and timber, Linlithgow Peel stood the test better than most masonry castles and stayed in English hands until after Bannockburn in 1314. Even

then it was only taken by a cunning ruse when a local man, William Bunnock, hid eight armed men in his hay-cart and halted it right in the middle of the gateway to prevent the portcullis from being lowered. The peel survived until 1424 when a great fire swept through the town and destroyed the peel and ancient royal seat.

The second significant survival is Lochmaben Castle, Dumfriesshire. We know that the English built a peel there in 1298, which changed hands several times before being taken back by the English in 1333. The strength then remained in enemy hands until Archibald 'the Grim' finally retook it for Scotland in 1385, the last English outpost other than Roxburgh remaining on Scottish soil. It was during these last decades of English occupation that major works were carried out at the garrison, as the excavations carried out there in the 1970s confirmed. The works included the refortification of the old peel, possibly so that it could be used as a protected work camp for the 'stonemasons, carpenters and other workmen' labouring on the imposing stone front rising up behind.

There may have been another type of English stronghold built in Scotland but which has to date escaped detection – temporary camps for the king and his retinue while on campaign. As Edward I led his field army about the country he normally availed himself of captured castles and compliant monasteries for his temporary quarters; that is how he came to be at Kildrummy and Dunfermline. But there may well have been occasions when this proved impracticable. After capturing Caerlaverock in July 1300, Edward continued on his invasion of Galloway and remained for a short while at Girthon, west of Kirkcudbright. But where precisely? Was it the motte castle now in the woods behind Cally House, or could the nearby earthwork (now intriguingly known as 'Palace Yard') have been built specifically for his use? It is a simple enough site, an oval area of ground enclosed by a bank and ditch; the bank was presumably palisaded.

Temporary residences

Bruce's policy of rendering captured castles incapable of further use certainly made life more difficult for the English in the shorter term, but where were those lords whose castles had been 'razed to the ground' expected to reside thereafter? Such was the predicament faced in 1337 by Sir Andrew Moray of Bothwell, the grand-nephew of William 'the Rich', when, having just wrested his ancestral castle back from the enemy, he yielded to the patriotic necessity of pulling down one half of his mighty donjon (see **colour plate 4**). The short answer is that we have no real idea. Some castles may have been repaired. Tree-ring dating of the bridge timbers at Caerlaverock has shown that the original bridge of the 1270s was patched up in the 1330s, but this coincides with Edward Balliol's arrival on the scene and with Sir Eustace Maxwell of Caerlaverock's change of allegiance (yet again) – he repaired and garrisoned the castle before placing it at Balliol's disposal. And so the question still remains: where had Sir Eustace and his household been living for the preceding twenty years, since 1312 in fact, when he had received financial reward from Robert Bruce 'for demolishing the castle'?

It is just possible that the nobility abandoned their great stone castles while hostilities lasted and withdrew to less substantial residences of earth and timber. These are likely to have taken the form of moated manors, which were reasonably cheap and quick to construct but which offered a measure of defence against limited attack. The internal buildings would not have been anywhere near as grand as those they had recently abandoned.

That such residences were perfectly acceptable to the senior nobility is demonstrated by the action of King Robert Bruce himself. In 1326 the ageing monarch acquired an estate at Cardross, on the opposite bank of the River Leven to the royal castle of Dumbarton. There he had a manor house built which became his home. It contained a hall, chambers for the king and Queen Elizabeth, a chapel, kitchen and

larder. We read in the records of plastered and painted walls, glazed windows and thatched roofs. Beyond the confines of the house there was a garden, and a park where the king indulged his passion for hunting and falconry. It was at Cardross that he died three years later.

The motte castle seems also to have made a come-back during this troubled time. It was, after all, conditions such as the Scots were now experiencing that had created the motte in the first place. Like the moated manor, it was quick and inexpensive to construct (assuming that the lord had plenty of cheap labour at his disposal), but its extra height improved its defensive capability. Unexpected confirmation that mottes were still being constructed in Scotland in the early fourteenth century came in the 1970s during excavation of a motte near Roberton in Upper Clydesdale (**33**). Pottery found beneath the mound unequivocally ruled out Robert the Fleming in the mid-twelfth century as its builder, and instead pointed to Mary of Stirling as the person responsible. Mary's allegiance had been with the Balliols throughout the troubles but in 1346 she felt it necessary to resign her Roberton lands in the hope of securing a pardon from David II. The little motte overlooking a winding in the River Clyde seems to have been her way of defending herself and those in her service at such a critical time.

We saw earlier (page 22) that many of the 300-odd mottes recorded in Scotland are to be found in Galloway and Moray, and that hitherto this concentration has been put down to the fact that both regions were distinctly hostile to the crown in the twelfth and early thirteenth centuries. But both areas were also very turbulent during the early fourteenth century when the conflict was as much a civil war as a war of independence, with The Bruce and his supporters set against Balliol's henchmen. With Roberton now dated to the early fourteenth century, it begs the question just how many other mottes in these regions might conceivably be of the same vintage. The oft-used distribution map of Scottish mottes may be more misleading than revealing.

33 Roberton Motte, near Biggar, Lanarkshire, under excavation in 1978. Several of the post-holes holding the timber palisade encircling the summit of the mound are visible in the foreground. From the old ground surface beneath the motte (see the large trench into the heart of the mound in the background) came pottery which dated its construction to no earlier than 1300.

After the wars were over

The return to Scotland in 1357 of King David II, Robert Bruce's son, from lengthy captivity in England effectively ended the bloody wars with England. A greater part of the country had effectively been free of the English aggressor for some time, particularly the north and west, although a large swathe of the south of Scotland still remained under their control, ruled from the castles at Roxburgh and Lochmaben. The return of a sort of peace was the time for all to rebuild their lives, and their homes.

In all wars there are winners and losers. In the wars with England the losers were the Balliols and their supporters, particularly the Comyns. The winners were those who had sided with Bruce, like the Stewarts, the MacDonalds and the Douglases. The Douglases had been quite modest Lanarkshire landowners in the thirteenth century, but the close friendship between 'the Good' Sir James Douglas and Robert Bruce himself secured their rise to the top. Through him they acquired substantial estates across the land, among them the barony of North Berwick, on the East Lothian coast. Sir James' beneficiary at his death in 1330 was his nephew, William. It was he who built mighty Tantallon Castle (**colour plate 7**).

Tantallon – last of the great curtain-wall castles

The motive for William embarking on such a mammoth undertaking may have been prompted by his elevation to the peerage as the first earl of Douglas in 1358; certainly the castle has the hallmark of being a declaration of his new-found status. It was as if William Douglas consciously chose to look back to the golden age of castle building in the preceding century, and Tantallon can claim to be the last of the great curtain-walled castles built 'from new' in Scotland.

The most important and conspicuous element in Tantallon's design was the awesome curtain of red sandstone drawn across the neck of the grassy headland (**34**). Impressively solid behind its yawning rock-cut ditch, it now has a somewhat careworn appearance, having been

34 The awesome curtain wall at Tantallon Castle, near North Berwick, East Lothian, built about 1360 by William, first earl of Douglas, rears up behind the outer entrance gate and gun tower built by Archibald Douglas, sixth earl of Angus, prior to King James V's great siege in 1528.

battered not only by cannon but by the winds and storms that are as much a part of this exposed spot as the rugged cliffs themselves. The brute frontal mass of the curtain has just a few narrow slits lighting the wall chambers and access stairs behind. Three towers projecting from the great curtain provided the main residential accommodation. The central tower housed the gateway at ground level and four upper floors, part of which would almost certainly have been occupied by the constable. The north tower, known as the Douglas Tower, is of such a size (it had seven floors) that it must have been the earl's residence, his donjon. This is confirmed by the presence immediately behind it of a two-storey hall block, originally provided with halls on both floors, a great hall on the upper floor reserved for the lord's use, and a laigh (lower) hall for less-exalted gatherings. In essence, Tantallon was a Bothwell or a Kildrummy adapted to a promontory site, nothing more, nothing less.

Tantallon was quite exceptional, and we shall never really know what motivated the earl of Douglas to build in the manner and on the scale that he did. In so doing he was out of step with his peers, who were demonstrating a preference for a less ambitious and less costly residence, centred on the tower house. Even William himself at another of his seats, Hermitage, close by the Border with England, opted for the latest fashion, albeit in a rather unusual way.

Tall storeys – the re-emergence of the tower house

There was nothing new about the tower house. The stone towers that had sprung up in Orkney and Caithness in the twelfth century, and the timber towers that had been erected in ringworks and atop mottes across the rest of the country, had led the way. The squat stone tower built on the summit of the motte at Duffus in the early fourteenth century may simply have been a recreation in masonry of its timber predecessor. Perhaps our perception of the tower house as essentially a product of the fourteenth century is coloured by the surviving upstanding stone masonry. If all those timber towers built in the twelfth and thirteenth centuries had survived, would we now be talking of a new direction in castle-building, or simply of a new material for constructing them?

It may be that the free-standing tower as a lordly residence never actually declined during the thirteenth century, as has been claimed, but simply that certain of the senior nobility were persuaded to build anew in the grand manner. Perhaps we should not be asking why the tower house re-emerged in the fourteenth century but why the curtain-walled castle went out of favour so soon? Various theories have been advanced for the resurgence of the tower house, including financial impoverishment following years of war, the 'down-sizing' of baronial households, and the failure of the mighty castles to withstand siege. Perhaps the answer is a combination of all three, and others besides.

The prevailing view of the tower-house castle is of a lofty, isolated dwelling housing all its lord's residential needs. If the tower was accompanied at all by other buildings, these were in the nature of 'farmyard attachments' and not buildings which any self-respecting lord would deign to enter. Such a picture might be a more accurate reflection of the tower houses of the sixteenth and seventeenth centuries, when the social order was very different, but it cannot be sustained for those erected in the fourteenth and fifteenth centuries. Once again, the misconception is brought about by our obsession with the upstanding masonry, and our failure to take into account what has vanished from our sight and is now only recoverable through excavation. To quote an old adage: absence of evidence is not necessarily evidence of absence.

The impression of the fourteenth-century tower-house castle as 'a closed-up, inward-

35 Hallforest Castle, near Kintore, Aberdeenshire, from the north, painted by James Giles in the early nineteenth century.

looking building' is certainly reinforced at Hallforest (Aberdeenshire), one of the earliest of the 'new' stone tower houses (35). The gaunt, oblong structure rises 20m (66ft) above the level ground about it. Within its 2m (6ft) thick walls were six floors of accommodation. The present ruin gives no clue as to how the tower was entered but an eighteenth-century account tells of a ladder reaching to the second floor. Internally there is no sign of a stair, and access through the building must have been by timber ladders and hatches through the floors. Two stone vaults divided the tower into three distinct units. The bottom two floors beneath the lower vault housed a cellar and kitchen; the middle two floors beneath the upper vault provided a hall and withdrawing room above; the top two floors may have formed the lord's private apartment, including his bedchamber. This was the stock recipe normally used by builders of

tower houses throughout the fourteenth and fifteenth centuries.

The builder of Hallforest was very probably Sir Robert Keith, who through his association with Bruce had benefited substantially following the forfeiture of John Comyn, earl of Buchan, in 1308. He therefore had considerable wealth; he also had power and prestige through his office of marischal (marshal) of Scotland. Hallforest may not have been his principal residence, but given the likely extent of his travelling household, perhaps numbering about fifty, can we really see this solitary tower as the full extent of his castle on his Kintore estate? Without excavation, of course, we cannot say, but excavation beside another imposing fourteenth-century tower house, Threave, strongly suggests that it wasn't.

Excavations at Threave

The tall, forbidding tower that dominates the little island of Threave in the Kirkcudbrightshire Dee on which it stands, is the most impressive of all these early towers (36). It was built for Archibald Douglas 'the Grim' (so-called by the English, it was said, 'becaus of his terrible countenance in weirfair') following his elevation to the lordship of Galloway in 1369.

Before the excavations in the 1970s, the prevailing view of the castle in which Archibald, by now third earl of Douglas, died on Christmas Eve 1400 was of a mighty tower house standing in splendid isolation on its island – 'a tower and nothing but a tower'. There is no escaping the fact that it must have been a very imposing residence in its heyday. It stood 30m (98ft) high, with walls 3m (10ft) thick, and housed five floors of accommodation, arranged similarly to those at Hallforest with kitchen, prison, well and storage at the bottom, a hall in the middle and private chambers above – in all 450sq m (nearly 5,000sq ft) of living space. But was this sufficient for someone of Archibald Douglas's standing, who at his death was the most powerful nobleman in southern Scotland? How, for example, did it compare with the amount of accommodation available to his cousin, William Douglas, at Tantallon? The answer is: very badly. A conservative estimate of the floor space at Tantallon, counting only those buildings currently standing, the three curtain-wall towers

and the hall block, comes to about 1,100sq m (12,000sq ft), well over double that at Threave. Not only that, but the amount available in the Douglas Tower at Tantallon, identified as the earl's private lodging within the castle, adds up to 450sq m (5,000sq ft), the same as Threave. Were we then missing something at the latter?

The excavations clearly showed that we were. Under the grass to the east of the tower house, within metres of Archibald's front door, were found the masonry foundations of two substantial structures of fourteenth-century date. Both were interpreted as being of two storeys, in which case taken together they add a further 600sq m (6,500sq ft) of living space, thereby matching almost exactly the provision at Tantallon. The excavations by no means exhausted all the extra accommodation around the tower house, just as at Tantallon there must be more to be found.

36 Threave Castle, near Castle Douglas, Kirkcudbrightshire, from the north-east in 1976. The two buildings found close beside Archibald the Grim's tower house were built contemporaneously with the tower in the later fourteenth century but were demolished about 1450 to make room for the new artillery fortification that was wrapped around the tower house.

37 Plan of Finlaggan, the island residence of the MacDonald
Lords of the Isles on Islay, Argyllshire.

The excavations did not permit the functions of the two buildings to be identified, but by analogy with other sites such as Archibald's other chief seat at rebuilt Bothwell, we might postulate a great hall for the one and extra lodging space, including possibly a chapel, for the other. Black Archibald's residence now takes on a very different appearance to the lonely tower house there today. Thanks to the excavations we can picture most of the habitable part of the island crammed with buildings, two of which at least were of high status (colour plate 8). In this regard the castle complex begins to take on an appearance similar to that at Finlaggan, the principal residence on Islay of the MacDonald Lords of the Isles, who rose to prominence about the same time as the Douglases (37). There two islands linked by a causeway were crowded with an assortment of buildings, including over twenty on the larger Eilean Mór. The only significant difference between the two complexes is the nature of the lord's private residence which at Finlaggan seems not to have been a tower house.

Threave and the other fourteenth-century towers like Hallforest might now be seen in a different light from hitherto – not so much castles in their own right but private lodgings reserved for the lord's own use, and the last resort in times of trouble, set within a much larger complex which more sensibly matches our understanding of the nature of baronial obligations and the size and scale of their households. We might reasonably christen them tower-house castles to distinguish them from the curtain-walled castles of the preceding century. In the latter the dominating feature had been the mighty enclosing wall, and the accommodation, with the exception of the great hall, had been firmly embedded within it. In the tower-house castle the curtain was reduced to a perimeter wall of middling strength playing second fiddle to the lordly accommodation. The perfect illustration of this is Doune Castle.

Doune – the perfect tower-house castle

Doune, beside the River Teith 12km (7½ miles) north-west of Stirling, was built towards the end of the century by Robert Stewart, first duke of Albany, earl of Menteith and Fife, and the younger brother of Robert III. From 1388 until his death in 1420 he was the effective ruler of the kingdom, and his seat at Doune virtually a royal castle. What we see there today was planned and executed in a single building programme, though the original scheme was never fully completed (colour plate 9).

Albany's vision was of four ranges of buildings set around a central court. The principal range along the north and north-west sides was to dominate all else. To achieve this it took the place of the perimeter wall, while the other ranges were to be built against the inside face of that defensive wall in the more traditional manner. This main range is as perfect a piece of medieval castle planning as one will find anywhere. A lofty tower, the gate tower, at the east end provided the duke and duchess with a spacious four-storey apartment, similar in size to Threave. It had its own defended entrance from the courtyard, and independent access from its first-floor hall into the dais end of the great hall to its west. The voluminous great hall itself, set upon cavernous storage vaults, had a separate entrance at its lower 'screens' end. Adjacent to the great hall, and linked to it by a servery, was the kitchen tower, more modest in size than the gate tower but housing an impressive kitchen on the first floor and two floors of respectable lodging space above. Interestingly, the amount of floor space in the range totals some 1,100sq m (12,000sq ft), identical to that at Tantallon and Threave.

It is Doune's cathedral-like great hall which impresses most today (38). It measures 170sq m (1,830sq ft) and rises 11m (36ft) to the apex of the roof. There are no fireplaces, so iron braziers must have heated the assembled throng summoned to sup with Albany, a man noted for his 'large tabling and belly cheer'. Its existence is a reminder of the continuing, pivotal importance of the great hall in castle planning.

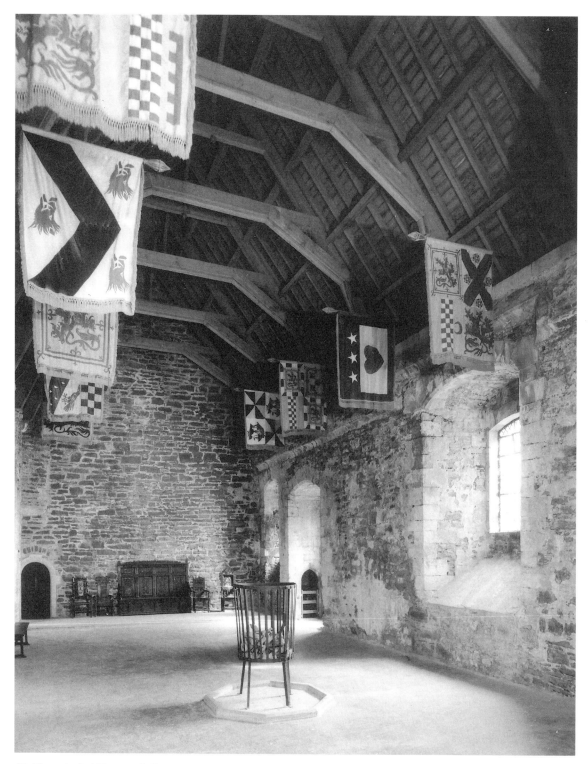

38 The cathedral-like great hall in Doune Castle, Perthshire. The room was restored, and the present roof put on, by the fourteenth earl of Moray in 1883, but evidence existed for the central brazier stance and the round-headed doorway at the far end, the dais end, which led to Albany's private apartment in the tower house beyond.

1 Edinburgh Castle Rock from the south, with the River Forth and Fife in the background. Recent archaeological excavations have shown that the Rock was inhabited at least as early as the late Bronze Age (about 900 BC).

2 Barmagachan Motte, Kirkcudbrightshire: a fairly typical Scottish example being small, created from a natural rock outcrop, and about which scarcely anything is known.

3 Castle Sween, Argyllshire, with Jura and Mull in the distance. The residence built by Suibhne, progenitor of the MacSween family, in the late twelfth century, is now the oldest standing castle in Scotland.

4 Bothwell Castle, Lanarkshire, with the River Clyde below. The mighty donjon of the Morays, built in the later thirteenth century but partially destroyed during the Wars of Independence, is justly recognized as the finest piece of medieval secular architecture surviving in Scotland.

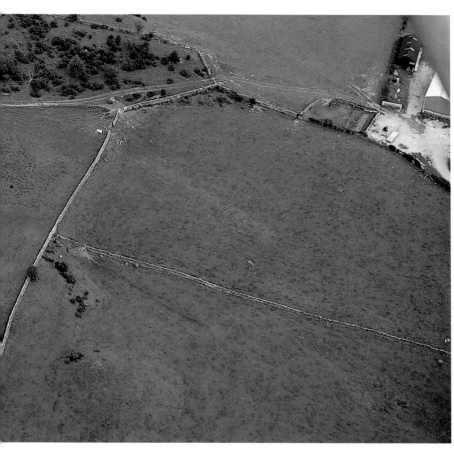

5 Gelston Moat, Kirkcudbrightshire, is barely visible from the ground but the two rectangular platforms on which the manor buildings were built can be made out from the air.

6 The siege of Caerlaverock, 1300, drawn by David Simon. Full details of the two-day investment by the English of Lord Maxwell's stronghold beside the Solway Firth were recorded in a contemporary account, the *Roll of Karlaverock*.

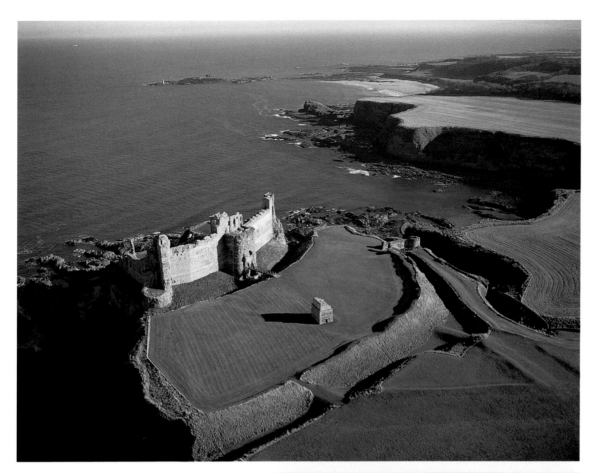

7 Tantallon Castle, East Lothian, from the air, a
fortress-residence of the Douglases for 400 years.
The basic layout of two large courts, the inner court
shielded behind the awesome stone curtain wall,
dates from the beginnings of the castle's occupation
in the mid-fourteenth century, whereas the lonely
dovecot in the outer ward and the triangular ravelin
in the bottom right-hand corner belong to the
twilight of the castle's days as a lordly residence in
the seventeenth century.

8 An impression of how Threave Island,
Kirkcudbrightshire, might have looked at the time of
Archibald the Grim's death there in 1400, based on
the excavated evidence and drawn by David Simon.
This image of a bustling island community contrasts
dramatically with the present perception of an
isolated tower house.

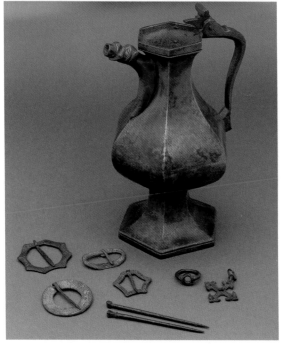

9 The courtyard and north range at Doune Castle, Perthshire. On the right was the lord's lodging, in the centre his great hall, and on the left a second tower housing a kitchen and other residential accommodation.

10 A fifteenth-century brass ewer and assorted jewellery discovered at Urquhart Castle, Inverness-shire, in the 1920s.

11 A wooden platter, bowl and paddle-blade found in the harbour mud at Threave Castle in 1976.

12 An impression of how the Halyburtons' residence in Dirleton Castle, East Lothian, might have looked in 1450, drawn by David Simon.

13 An impression of how Sir James Hamilton of Finnart's masterpiece, Craignethan Castle, Lanarkshire, might have looked in 1550, drawn by Tom Borthwick.

14 Castle Stalker, on Eilean an Stalcaire ('Hunter's Island'), Argyllshire, built about 1540 by Alan Stewart of Appin, a descendant of the former Stewart lords of Lorn, and one among many tower houses built throughout the land during the course of the sixteenth century.

15 Claypotts Castle, Angus, built for John Strachan in the aftermath of the Reformation in 1560.

The great hall at Darnaway

The number of more-or-less complete great halls surviving in Scotland can be counted on the fingers of one hand, and even that at Doune owes its present appearance to the intervention of the fourteenth earl of Moray in the 1880s, who restored it. By happy coincidence there exists at the earl of Moray's main seat, Darnaway (Morayshire), one of only two medieval great halls in the country still with its original roof (the other is in Edinburgh Castle).

The roof over 'Randolph's Hall' at Darnaway used to be ascribed on art-historical grounds to the 1450s, but recent dendrochronological dating has unequivocally placed its construction in the year 1387, making it earlier than the great hammer-beam roof over Westminster Hall, London, by several years (**39**). The owner of Darnaway at the time was John Dunbar, earl of

Moray and a brother-in-law of the king. The roof is a marvellous example of medieval craftsmanship. Its unusual hammer-beam form is enlivened with carved decoration. Two of the seven principal trusses are elaborately ornamented, possibly indicating the positions of partitions or screens in the open hall, demarcating the dais and service areas. In addition, there is a wealth of carving – human figures, birds and beasts – inhabiting the structure. Of particular interest are the human figures on the ends of some of the hammer beams. These include two crowned male heads facing each other on the principal truss, a pair

39 Part of the hammer-beam roof over 'Randolph's Hall' at Darnaway Castle, near Forres, Morayshire, whose great oak trusses have been dated by dendrochronology to the year 1387, making it earlier than the great roof over Westminster Hall, London, by several years.

40 The pair of cloaked and hooded clerics carved on one of the hammer-beam ends in 'Randolph's Hall', Darnaway.

The importance of the horse is evident through the abundance of horse trappings, like prick- and rowel-spurs, harness pendants, bits and shoes, and exceptionally the leather saddle-cloth from the moat at Caerlaverock (41). Horses were used for work and leisure more than they were for war, and many of the arrowheads found would have been for use in the hunt rather than in fighting. Dice, chess-pieces and counters illustrate other leisure pursuits. Military equipment, though, is represented by sword fragments, leather scabbards and chain mail. Other items of personal equipment frequently found include knives and daggers, spoons, personal seal matrices and assorted items of jewellery.

One of the finest objects recovered is the brass ewer from Urquhart Castle (**colour plate 10**). Such water jugs would have been a common sight in Scotland's castles for they were used to wash one's hands prior to sitting down to a meal. They stood over a flat-bottomed bowl on a side-table beside the doorway into the hall. In many surviving castle halls one can still see the slop-drain that took the waste out through the castle wall. Other household artefacts commonly found include barrel padlocks, keys of various kinds, candle holders and oil-lamp bowls, iron and bronze cauldrons, pottery and other vessels of glass and, very occasionally, of wood. Undoubtedly the finest collection of wooden bowls and plates came from the little harbour at Threave, several of them bearing the Douglas 'heart' branded into their bases (**colour plate 11** and **42**).

Thanks to its waterlogged conditions, which ensured the survival of organic as well as inorganic material, Threave harbour produced a far more representative sample of castle artefacts than any other Scottish castle. The picture that emerged from the harbour mud and from elsewhere on the island was of a community largely self-sufficient in the production of wooden objects, leather goods, iron, lead and even glass. Interestingly, given the predominance of the material at other

of cloaked and hooded clerics part way down (40), and, 'below the salt', a lustful male, with a twinkle in his eye and an erect penis, gazing across the hall into the doleful eyes of the welcoming sow opposite!

All in all, the roof is a remarkable legacy, giving us a fascinating glimpse into the Scotland of Archibald 'the Grim' and his contemporaries. It is a comfort to know that after almost a century of war with England the Scots had lost neither their sense of humour, nor their love of nature!

Artefacts and aspects of castle life

The carved heads in 'Randolph's Hall' represent one insight into castle life; artefacts recovered from below the ground during excavation shed light on others.

41 The piece of leather saddle-cloth, decorated with two 'green men', recovered in 1961 from the inner moat at Caerlaverock Castle.

42 A Douglas 'heart' branded into the underside of a wooden platter found in the harbour mud at Threave Castle in 1974. This armorial device was adopted by the family in recognition of 'the Good' Sir James of Douglas's exploits with the heart of his close friend, King Robert Bruce, following the monarch's death in 1329.

excavations, the islanders seemed to have little need of pottery.

From the harbour mud at Threave emerged another type of artefact, and in quantity; it was also one stock item that had to be brought in from a distance. The thirty-four stone cannonballs that were found there serve to illustrate that life on the island, indeed throughout Scotland, was to be vulnerable to a new threat as the new century dawned.

4
The coming of the gun: the fifteenth century

In that year [1436], King James raised a very strong army and besieged Roxburgh Castle about the beginning of the month of August. There were in number more than two hundred thousand men-at-arms. But they waited there a fortnight doing nothing worth recording because of a detestable split and most unworthy difference arising from jealousy; so, after losing all their fine large guns, both cannon and mortars, and gunpowder and carriages and wagons and many other things utterly indispensable for a siege, they returned home most ingloriously without effecting their object.

A new menace

The account of James I's abortive attempt to wrest Roxburgh Castle back from the English, described in the near-contemporary *Book of Pluscarden*, is clearly greatly exaggerated; we cannot imagine for one moment that a fifth of the entire population of the country was at the siege! Also, the impression given of a mighty artillery train seems to be hyperbole for the sake of effect. But that the Scots had guns at their disposal on that occasion is not in dispute.

Gunpowdered artillery, whereby a tube-shaped weapon used gunpowder to discharge a missile, had appeared in western Europe by the early fourteenth century and the Scots were not slow in realizing its potential. Primitive pieces might have been among the armament deployed against Dundarg Castle (Aberdeenshire) in 1334

and Stirling Castle in 1337. Before the end of the century Edinburgh Castle, by then already the location of a small armaments industry making bows, crossbows and siege engines, seems also to be emerging as an arsenal for the new-fangled weapon; in 1384 'an instrument called a gun' was purchased for the fortress together with quantities of sulphur and saltpetre for making the gunpowder.

By now an 'arms race' was developing across the states and principalities of western Europe in which the Scottish monarchs played their part. By the time of James II's death in 1460 at yet another siege of Roxburgh, this one ultimately successful, the royal artillery train was considerable, pride of place going to a giant siege gun, or bombard, called 'Mons' (or Mons Meg as she came to be known), gifted in 1457 by the king's uncle-by-marriage, Duke Phillip of Burgundy (**43**). But bombards proved to be inordinately cumbersome beasts, both to trundle about the country (Mons could cover only 5km (3 miles) a day) as well as to fire (Mons fired perhaps eight stones a day, such was the enormous heat generated in her breech after each firing). Their transportation was also a huge drain on resources. As a result, by the end of the fifteenth century the bombard had effectively been pensioned off (Mons became a ceremonial saluting gun) and replaced by smaller, more manageable pieces. Even then, the gun cannot be said to have achieved final supremacy over the more conventional

43 Mons Meg with some of her gunstones, on display in Edinburgh Castle. The mighty muzzle-loaded bombard weighed over 6040kg (6 tons) and fired gunstones weighing 150kg (350lbs) a distance of almost 3km (2 miles). The present wooden carriage is a twentieth-century creation; Mons, when in action, would probably have been laid on a solid wooden trestle.

armament until well into the sixteenth century. Nevertheless, as the fifteenth century wore on, builders of castles had no option but to take the new firearm into account.

Peace with security

This talk of guns might lead the reader into thinking that the Scots throughout the later Middle Ages were constantly at war, either with each other or with the English. This is after all the traditional, post-Jacobite, view of late medieval Scotland, as a country of 'barborous Scots' riven by 'the usual amount of feudal tyranny, violations of law and outrages on humanity'. However, this perception of a

country torn apart by outbreaks of violence, wherein feeble kings failed to control their overbearing barons, is simply not borne out by the facts, as Grant has recently demonstrated: 'Between 1341 and 1469 no Scottish king was overthrown by political opponents, whereas two were in England; England experienced twice as many rebellions and three times as many civil war battles; and three times as many English magnates met politically-related deaths, although the Scottish and English magnate classes were much the same size.'

That the Scots continued to build castles long after most of their English counterparts had ceased to do so has been taken as confirmation that Scottish domestic politics was far more turbulent than that prevailing south of the Border. This corresponds neatly with the widely held belief that all castles were built in times of trouble, that they were primarily defensive. But can we really sustain the argument that life was so troubled in late-medieval Scotland that many landowners were forced to build costly stone

77

fortified residences solely in order to defend themselves and those in their charge?

Looking down the other end of the telescope it could as easily be argued that the castle-building boom of the fifteenth century was rather more a reflection of the country's political stability and of the growing confidence of the nobility in its future. Building in stone and lime was a specialized, and costly, operation, not something that could be undertaken in haste. It required a considerable investment of capital spread over a number of years. No self-respecting nobleman was going to rush into such a venture unless he had a reasonable prospect of seeing it completed and thereafter enjoying the fruits of his endeavours. For that he needed settled political conditions and confidence that he had secure title to the land. The late-medieval castle, far from being regarded as an indicator of a disordered society, should more realistically be seen as a sign of peace and prosperity, where a nobleman's concern was as much for prestige and comfort as it was for security.

The rise of the middling sort

The building of costly stone residences had up till then largely been the preserve of the monarchy and the senior nobility. It has been estimated that of the 2,000 heads of noble families in Scotland in about 1300, no more than fifty could be counted as magnates. The remainder, while still classed as nobility, would be more accurately termed 'landed gentry'. But by 1400 the picture was changing. The crown, for example, was already eroding the power of the provincial earldoms and important lordships that had dominated society up till then, and an act of 1401 ensured that when these came into the crown's possession, any baronies within them would henceforth be held directly of the crown. The number of 'tenants-in-chief' increased as a result.

This rise of the middling sort throughout the fifteenth century is reflected in the castle boom. More and more landowners, emboldened through their elevated status as tenants of the crown and encouraged by the knowledge that they held their land 'in feu and heredity and in perpetuity', now chose to 'move up-market' and invest their capital in new buildings. There was no legal impediment preventing them from doing so; in Scotland all freeholders were noblemen and equal under the law. The only social barrier to their building a stone castle seems to have been a financial one.

Cardoness – a typical tower house

The majority of these new castles took the lofty tower-house form rather than that of the more modest hall-house variety. Cardoness Castle (Kirkcudbrightshire), built about 1475 by the McCullochs, a powerful Galloway family, was typical (**44**). The rectangular building rose 17m (56ft) to the battlements. Once through the ground-level front door one was confronted with six floors of accommodation arranged in a similar fashion to that at Threave, that is, service rooms at the bottom, a fine lord's hall in the middle, and private chambers at the top. These were reached by a spiral stair placed beside the entrance at one corner of the rectangle. Clever use was made of the 3m (10ft) thick walls to carve out small side chambers at every level. These served a variety of uses, including a guard room, a prison and pit, and several closets for use either as bed-chambers, wardrobes or latrines. The hall was particularly finely detailed, with an attractive fireplace, exquisite aumbry (cupboard) where the laird's finest plate would be displayed, and pretty stone window-seats. The available floor space amounted to about 320sq m (3,444sq ft), two-thirds that of Threave, reflecting the more lowly status of its owner.

Cardoness does not stand alone but has the remains of buildings surviving in its shadow. It is impossible to determine what function they served but my guess is that one would have been a great hall, to complement the provision within the tower house. The lordly obligations of the McCullochs would not have been as onerous or as elaborate as those of someone like Archibald 'the

44 An impression of how the tower house in Cardoness Castle, near Gatehouse-of-Fleet, might have been used by the MacCulloch family in the later fifteenth century. Drawn by David Simon.

Grim', but that would not have removed the necessity for such a public reception space. Archaeological evidence from two other tower-house castles in southern Scotland, Crichton and Smailholm, confirms that these later tower houses, even those belonging to quite modest lairds, were not intended to house all the noble functions.

Towers and halls

The hall (*aula*), the principal reception room in a nobleman's house, had been at the heart of castle planning from the very outset. That it continued to play an important part in late-medieval castle planning in Scotland is attested in both the surviving documentation – the phrase 'to build a house with a hall' occurs in about fifty feu charters during James IV's reign (1488–1513) – and the standing buildings themselves, most notably the monumentally impressive great hall built in the 1420s by James I as the centrepiece of his new stone palace at Linlithgow. The hall provided a suitably impressive space in which its lord could carry out his courtly and social obligations; more than any other room in the castle complex, it reflected in its size and ornamentation its owner's standing and aspirations.

Crichton Castle (Midlothian), perched on a bracken-covered terrace overlooking the marshy haugh through which the River Tyne twists and turns, was built most probably by John de Crichton, who died in 1406 (**45**). His tower house was subsequently reduced in height by one storey and enveloped by later buildings which largely superseded the original tower house as the lordly accommodation. Of particular interest are the pit-prison and poky kitchen squeezed into the bottom two floors, and the two entrance doorways, one above the other, the lower one giving access into the service basement and the upper one entering directly into the third-floor hall and presumably reached by a timber forestair.

The north range in Crichton Castle, abutting the tower, is now justly celebrated for its sumptuous late sixteenth-century architecture

45 An impression of Crichton Castle, near Pathhead, Midlothian, as it might have looked in 1400 when first built. Drawn by David Simon.

and planning. However, the lower parts of the walls along the north, west and south are clearly of earlier date, and excavation in the 1980s confirmed the former existence of the east wall. The evidence points to the structure having been a two-storey hall block adjacent to, and complementing the accommodation in, the tower house. The amount of floor space available to de Crichton would have almost doubled as a result, from 240 to 430sq m (2,580 to 4,630sq ft). The presence of the hall block also explains the somewhat eccentric siting of the castle well in the later complex.

Smailholm Tower (Roxburghshire) was probably built about the middle of the century by the Pringles. The head of the family was a squire of the earl of Douglas and who managed a part of the Ettrick Forest on his lordship's behalf. The position brought with it both status and wealth, which perhaps explains why the family chose to build in costly stone and lime. Their modest, five-storey rectangular tower, providing 200sq m (2,150sq ft) of floor space, testifies to their more lowly lairdly status. However, recent excavation in the barmkin surrounding the tower house uncovered evidence for a hall block, in this case of single-storey height, to complement the cramped accommodation in the tower (**46**). The block consisted of a hall measuring 50sq m (538sq ft) nearer to the outer gateway, and a chamber half that size at the end closer to the tower house. The hall was heated by a brazier placed in the centre of the room, in a manner identical to the much grander great hall at Doune. Across the courtyard from the hall was the two-roomed kitchen block.

Until these excavations, the absence of kitchens within the tower houses themselves had been put down to several factors, most popular being the fire risk and the undesirable smells. Yet the tower houses of the senior nobility generally had kitchens; Archibald 'the Grim'

46 An impression of how the Pringles' residence at Smailholm Tower, near Kelso, Roxburghshire, might have looked in the later fifteenth century, based on the excavated evidence. The tower house itself, the family's private apartment, was complemented by an outer hall and kitchen in the west barmkin, just inside the outer gateway, and a little garden in the east barmkin. The stables and other outbuildings lay beyond the security of the barmkin wall. Intriguingly, no well was found anywhere within the walls. Drawn by David Simon.

evidently wasn't overly bothered about either going up in smoke or being overwhelmed by the stink of cabbage water wafting up the stairs! The more likely explanation for the lack of kitchens in the lesser tower houses, like Cardoness and Smailholm, is that, with space at a premium, the cooking of private family meals was done over the hall fire, as numerous contemporary woodcuts suggest (47), while more public feasts were catered for in the kitchen beside the outer hall.

The excavations at Threave demonstrated that the mighty tower house of a great late fourteenth-century magnate was but the central element in a much more elaborate complex of buildings, the lord's private residence and place of last resort. The excavations at Smailholm coupled with the observations at Crichton show how that same picture can be carried forward into the fifteenth century, and down the social ladder.

Variations on the tower-house theme

The single most appealing feature of the Scottish tower house as a building type is its considerable variety. Builders took the original simple rectangular form and stretched it, added to it and contorted it into all shapes and sizes. No two towers were identical, though they all had features in common. The castle 'boom' of the fifteenth century began this process of mutation in earnest, a development that lasted until well into the seventeenth century.

The tower houses that we have encountered up to now have all been of the rectangular form, and most tower houses built during the century were similarly contrived. The most common variation on this theme was the L-plan where a smaller jamb (or wing) was attached to one side of the main block. Depending on its size, the jamb could be used for a number of purposes. At Affleck Castle (Angus), built towards the end of the century by one of the Auchinleck family, the jamb was just a sixteenth the size of the main block and was utilized in its lower storeys for the main spiral stair giving access to the hall on the third floor (48). Thereafter, the

47 A woodcut of about 1500 showing the family meal being prepared in the hall fireplace.

stair to the upper levels and the battlements was carried up in a spiral contained in the thickness of one of the other corners leaving the remaining two floors of the jamb to be deployed as living space. The lower one, entered by steps off the hall, may have served as a bedchamber for the steward; the upper level, entered off the laird's private chamber, housed a lovely little chapel (49).

Affleck's plan is unusual for this period. The more normal arrangement was to apply a much bigger jamb to the main block and use the greater floor space to provide a more flexible arrangement of the accommodation. The tower house at Neidpath Castle (Peeblesshire), built at the beginning of the century by the Hays of Locherworth, ancestors of the earls of Tweeddale, had a jamb just one quarter the size of the main block. It was entirely devoted to living space, including a pit-prison at ground level, a store room on the first floor, a kitchen off the hall and private chambers on the top two levels.

48 Affleck Castle, north of Dundee, Angus, an early L-plan tower house, built by the Auchinleck family in the late fifteenth century.

49 Affleck's charming little chapel, entered off the laird's
private chamber.

One tower house, Orchardton Tower (Kirkcudbrightshire), was unique in Scotland in being circular in form, although the rooms inside were square on plan (50). The Cairns family who built it about the middle of the century must have had an Irish connection for the form is more common on the other side of the North Channel, for example Synone, County Tipperary. In all other respects Orchardton follows the standard layout of accommodation with a cellar at ground level (independently accessed), a hall on the first floor and private chambers above. Orchardton also provides a good example of the relationship between the private tower house and the more public hall block, which lies adjacent.

50 Orchardton Tower, the residence of the Cairns family near Dalbeattie, Kirkcudbrightshire. The tower's circular shape is unique in Scotland, but in most other respects the castle complex is typical. The round-headed doorway a third the way up the building gave access between the laird's apartment within the tower house and the more public outer hall and kitchen in the foreground.

Borthwick – a most unusual tower house

Of all the tower houses built during the century, one in particular, Borthwick Castle (Midlothian), stands out from the rest for a whole variety of reasons: for its monumental size – at a height of 36m (188ft) it was the loftiest; for its massive scale – with a total floor space in excess of 1,100sq m (12,000sq ft) it was the largest; for the supreme quality of its ashlar construction; and for the very clever arrangement of the accommodation (51). Sir William Borthwick, who in 1430 received a licence from James I 'to construct a castle ... and to erect and fortify the same', must have been pleased with what he built, and greatly admired (and envied) by his peers. Yet Sir William was only in the second rank of the nobility at the time he created it; it was to be twenty years before he was elevated to the new peerage established by James II and given the title of Lord Borthwick, thereby elevating him to the top rank. Evidently Sir William was a man determined to better himself.

The sheer volume of Borthwick strongly suggests that Sir William was contriving to bring

51 An aerial view from the south-east of Borthwick Castle and St Kentigern's Church, near Gorebridge, Midlothian. The splendid double tomb of a lord and his lady in the south chapel of the kirk is thought to be that of the first Lord Borthwick, and his good lady, who were the builders and first residents of the impressive tower.

all his lordly accommodation under one roof, rather than have two or perhaps three high-status buildings in close proximity to each other as Archibald 'the Grim' had produced at Threave. In this Sir William was not being entirely innovative. Hermitage Castle, begun by Archibald's cousin, William, first earl of Douglas, and completed by his successors before 1400 achieved a similar result, albeit by stages and not at one fell swoop. So too did the tower house built inside the twelfth-century ringwork at Crookston by Sir John Stewart of Darnley about 1400 (see 3); the date was confirmed during excavation in 1973 by the discovery of a silver groat of Robert III (1390–1406) in mint

condition in a construction trench for the tower house. Unfortunately for us, both these castles defy proper analysis; at Hermitage the 'restoration work' of the early nineteenth century removed much of the evidence, while at Crookston most of the main block and western towers have long since disappeared, possibly as a result of the punishment meted out by Mons Meg during the 1489 siege. Nevertheless, enough remains at both sites to hint that their central blocks housed the public rooms, including the great hall and withdrawing chamber, while the four projecting jambs, one at each corner, contained all the accommodation one would expect to find in a conventional tower house.

The arrangement at Borthwick is not so convoluted (52). The main block had just two jambs projecting from it, both from the same side and flush with the gable walls to create a kind of E-plan without the central stem. The ground and first floors were taken up by store rooms. On the second floor was the splendid great hall (53), measuring 112sq m (1,200sq ft) and rising 10m (33ft) to the apex of its great stone vault, with the withdrawing chamber and kitchen in the two adjacent jambs. The upper floors comprised the lordly apartments, including a good-sized hall (as big and as impressive as one would find anywhere else in the country at the time) and a chapel.

Masons and their marks

Borthwick holds another potential treasure, for cut into its ashlar-block walls is a liberal sprinkling of masons' marks, over sixty different marks in total. I use the word 'potential' because to date there has been little research done on Scottish masons' marks. This is to be regretted for a more thorough analysis could achieve several ends. It could lead to a better building chronology within a specific castle, and it could link the construction of different buildings, not just castles, with the same group of masons. This rich potential has recently been ably demonstrated by Zeune, and what follows is the fruit of his research.

The masons' marks in Borthwick enabled the tower house to be analysed from bottom to top. Several facts emerged. Most significant was confirmation that the structure was of homogenous build. The spiral stairs, doors, windows, fireplaces, closets, vaults, the kitchen arch, the fireplace, basin and buffet in the great hall, the chapel, even the curb on the basement well, were all original. Only the odd window enlargement, door insertion, fireplace restoration, stair repair and garret rebuilding were shown to be of later date. Secondly, the individual mason was versatile, at one time producing a newel-tread for one of the spiral stairs, at another hewing an elaborately carved piece for the great hall buffet. The study also demonstrated that there was a fair amount of coming and going by the masons, including the interesting observation that for the construction of the impressive stone vault over the great hall several new masons were brought on site who worked on that one feature alone.

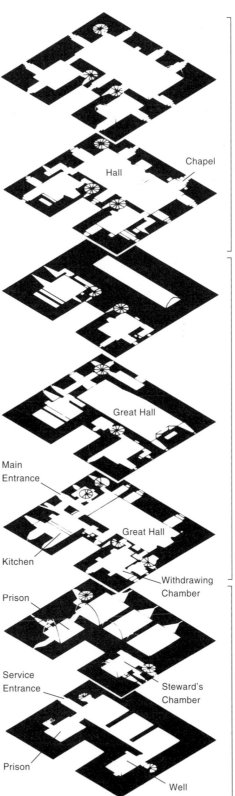

Lord and Lady Borthwick's private apartments including hall, chapel and chambers.

Chapel

Hall

Great hall, withdrawing chamber, kitchen and porter's lodge.

Great Hall

Main Entrance

Great Hall

Kitchen

Withdrawing Chamber

Prison

Service Entrance

Steward's Chamber

Service basement including steward's chamber, prisons, store rooms and well.

Prison

Well

52 The floor plans of Borthwick Castle.

53 A nineteenth-century engraving of the great hall in Borthwick Castle, looking towards the 'hie burde' end, with its grand fireplace, dais window (left) and elaborate buffet recess (right). The artist, Robert Billings, has used the fireplace hood to highlight the many masons' marks.

What then of the possibility of linking the masons who contributed to the building of Borthwick with other building projects? Zeune once again suggests some intriguing possibilities. Some twenty of the masons who created Roslin Chapel about 1450 had previously worked on Borthwick, perfectly understandable given the close proximity of the two sites and the fact that the building of the chapel followed neatly the completion of the castle. But other masons working on Roslin had travelled from much further afield, including several from Angus, where they had been engaged in building work at two castles, Airlie and Inverquharity, as well as Arbroath Abbey. From Roslin, masons travelled to a variety of building sites, including Melrose Abbey (Roxburghshire), Linlithgow Palace, Ravenscraig Castle and Rosyth Castle (both Fife), Dean Castle near Kilmarnock (Ayrshire) and the Campbell castle at Kilchurn on Loch Awe (Argyllshire).

Scarcely anything is known about the master-masons and masons themselves, or for that matter the army of joiners, slaters, glaziers, smiths and labourers who contributed so much to the castle boom of the fifteenth century. Even their names are a mystery. The only master-masons of this century known to us by name are Henry Merlion, who was engaged by the crown at Ravenscraig in the early 1460s, Walter Merlion, his son, who worked on Stirling Castle and the Palace of Holyroodhouse around the turn of the century, Andrew Aytoun, who was also employed at Stirling Castle, and the Frenchman, John Morow, who thoughtfully placed an account of his works, none of them castles apparently, on a wall in Melrose Abbey. The quality of their creations is testimony to their craftsmanship, the quantity to their hard work. The end of a finger discovered in 1974

between two stones forming the arched entranceway into the Hepburns' castle of Hailes, beside the East Lothian Tyne, is silent testimony to the fact that their working conditions were not without their hazards.

Home improvements

The masons and other craftsmen were engaged not only on building new stone castles but also on upgrading existing residences.

The most obvious candidates in urgent need of improvement were those mighty curtain-walled castles erected in the 'golden age' of the thirteenth century when great magnates had grand ideas – and required just as grand households to sustain them. By the fifteenth century, such residences were obsolete, the product of a bygone age, and more compact and comfortable lordly seats were increasingly the order of the day. They were also probably in need of urgent repair and attention, particularly given the punishment meted out to them during the bloody wars with England.

Take the Black Douglases, for example. Faced with the daunting prospect of rebuilding the shattered castle of Bothwell, acquired through marriage in the mid-fourteenth century, they ended up with a walled enclosure half the size of that originally contemplated by Walter of Moray, centred on a lofty tower house (now largely gone) and a great hall (largely complete to its wall-head) built during the time of Archibald, the fourth earl, in the early fifteenth century (**54**). Archibald's brother-in-law, Walter Halyburton, was similarly engaged in rebuilding an old fortress, Dirleton (see **19**), and he too chose to build an imposing tower-house residence in preference to the multi-towered complex of his illustrious de Vaux ancestor (**colour plate 12**). It remains one of the great tragedies in Scottish architectural history that so little survives of his creation. We are left only with the basement of his tower house, with its pretty chapel above a particularly grim prison and pit, the cavernous storage vaults (**55**) beneath his great hall, and

54 Bothwell Castle from the air, showing the extent of the late fourteenth-century Douglas castle in relation to that originally envisaged by Walter of Moray in the middle of the preceding century (see **14**). The Douglases' residence was centred on a lofty rectangular tower house and great hall (centre left). The mighty donjon of the Morays (right), badly damaged during the wars with England, was patched up and probably used for ancillary accommodation.

55 The cavernous storage vaults beneath the Halyburtons' residence in Dirleton Castle. Each storage bay was entered separately from the courtyard (left) through a securely barred doorway. The sheer size of these vaults hints at the lavish banquets that must have been held in the great hall above.

the cathedral-like kitchens. The great hall itself must have been a magnificent space if the stone buffet in the screens passage is anything to judge by.

Major rebuilding at the more venerable residences was motivated by necessity. A different motive lay behind home improvements to relatively new residences. No sooner had

William Crichton come into possession of the tower-house castle built by his father (see **45**) than he embarked on a scheme to improve it (**56**). The most important element in his new castle was a splendid great hall along the south side of the courtyard, with the main entrance and cellars at ground level and the hall itself on the upper floor (**57**). Crichton's motive can only have been a desire to display his own wealth and status, and he was very much a man on his way up in the world. A trusted servant of James I, by the time of the king's death in 1437 he had become sheriff of Edinburgh and keeper of the castle there. Two years later he was elevated to

56 An impression of Crichton Castle as it might have looked following Chancellor Crichton's remodelling of about 1450. (Compare this illustration with **45**.) Drawn by David Simon.

the prestigious position of chancellor. A fine new reception and banqueting hall in his late father's castle was surely his way of announcing to all and sundry that he had arrived at centre stage of Scottish political and social life. The equally impressive collegiate church he built nearby simply reinforced the message. This burning desire to flaunt new-found rank and status through new building was repeated by

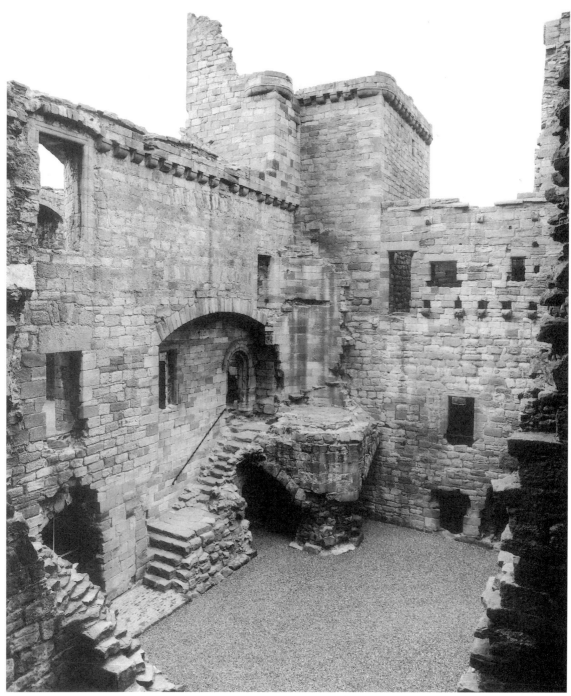

57 The courtyard facade (left) of Chancellor Crichton's great hall, viewed from within his father's tower house.

noblemen across the country. When, for example, Sir Andrew Lundy, lord of Balgonie Castle (Fife), was elevated to the post of lord high treasurer in 1496, he too marked the occasion by adding a new hall block to his family seat.

'All warlike apparatus for defence'

The impetus behind the castle boom might well have been the desire for prestige and comfort, but there was still the need for security. When William Keith, the marischal, embarked on his building of dramatic Dunnottar Castle (Kincardineshire) shortly before 1400 he wanted somewhere 'for the safe-keeping of his people and his goods'. A status symbol and somewhere warm were all well and good, but it wasn't all sweetness and light in late medieval Scotland, and in an age before banks were invented a nobleman's wealth had to be securely stored in his home.

The first licence to build a fortified residence was that granted by James I to James of Dundas of that Ilk and his heirs in 1424. Permission was given 'to build, construct, fortify and erect on high the tower or fortalice of Dundas in the manner of a castle with crenellations (*le kyrnelys*) and other manifestations below and above, with walls and ditches appropriate to this sort of fortalice, according to the custom of the kingdom of Scotland'. The tower house at Dundas Castle (West Lothian) stills stands almost in its entirety and is typical of the 'warlike apparatus' built into many of these fifteenth-century castles.

First, the tower house was built on the L-plan with the entrance door positioned in the re-entrant angle of the main block where it could be 'covered', that is protected, from the jamb. This use of the re-entrant angle to provide flanking defence became standard practice in later tower houses but was not always employed at this date. At Preston Castle (East Lothian), built by the Hamiltons in about 1450, the two superimposed entrances, one leading into the basement and the other giving access into the hall, were positioned on the opposite side of the main block from the jamb. The two superimposed entrances at Borthwick also ignored the defensive potential of the flanking jambs. Dundas's dependence on a ground-floor entrance was also not uniform at this date, though it became the norm later. Presumably the upper entrances at Borthwick and elsewhere were reached by timber forestairs, perhaps with a retractable element for better security (see **45**).

Most doorways at this date, wherever they were positioned in a building, were provided with two barriers, a wooden door and an iron yett (open cross-barred gate). In certain licences to fortify of about this date, including one granted to Herbert Lord Maxwell for Mearns Castle

(Renfrewshire) of 1449 and George, earl of Angus, for Broughty Castle (Angus) of 1454, special mention was made of these 'iron gates'. Usually they were placed behind the wooden door to strengthen it; less frequently they were placed at the front. Dundas still retains its iron yett.

The licences to fortify almost invariably highlight the importance of the wall-head. At Mearns, for instance, the laird was authorized 'to erect on the top of it all warlike apparatus necessary for its defence', and the surviving triple row of projecting corbels that once supported the oversailing parapet, evenly spaced to allow the defenders to fire down through the gaps, are testimony that Lord Maxwell carried out this particular letter of the law (**58**). This form of wall-head defence, called a machicolation, only began to come into fashion in Scotland in the early fifteenth century, to replace the timber hoards of the previous century, evidence for which can be seen at Threave (see **colour plate 8**) and Hermitage. Particularly fine machicolations may be seen on the top of the Douglas Tower in Bothwell Castle, built about 1420 by the fourth earl of Douglas, and on the inner curtain wall at Craigmillar Castle, the Prestons of Gorton's residence near Edinburgh (**59**). The dating of Craigmillar's machicolated wall remains a matter of debate (see pages 96–8), but somewhere around the middle of the fifteenth century seems the most likely.

Dundas also has a fine machicolation, but unlike the other examples quoted it also retains its crenellated, or indented, parapet, which was specifically mentioned in the licence. This was 'warlike apparatus' of long-standing, of course, and we have encountered earlier examples of the form at, for example, thirteenth-century Rothesay. However, we might question how necessary such elaborate wall-head defences were to James of Dundas and his peers. Did they really need to go to such lengths merely to ward off intruders and troublesome neighbours? Would not a simple parapet with a wall-walk behind, as at Neidpath, perhaps complemented

58 Mearns Castle, south-west of Glasgow, with its machicolated (slotted) wall-head defence still in place.

59 The inner curtain wall at Craigmillar Castle, Edinburgh, with its attractive machicolated parapet and projecting round towers fitted with gunholes.

by a projecting stone box placed on the wall-head directly over the entrance, as at Lochranza, have sufficed (**60**)? Although such battlements were built ostensibly for defence – and the licences confirm by their language this 'defensive' message – they seem unwarranted for the circumstances of the time and it may be argued that they were provided more for show than for strength. There is no doubting their eye-catching quality.

Threave and the arrival of artillery defence

The provision of wall-head defences, iron yetts and the like were all designed to counter the threat posed by conventional weapons, chiefly crossbows and stone-hurling artillery. From the middle of the century that situation began to change as the new firearm, the gun, started to come into its own. Certainly the warlike James II, by the time of his tragic death at Roxburgh in 1460, had built up a considerable artillery train, and there is clear evidence that some of his mightier subjects were similarly amassing arsenals. Foremost among them were the Black Douglases.

One of the greatest upheavals in fifteenth-century Scotland was the fall of the house of Black Douglas. Both during the years leading up to the dénouement in 1455 and in its aftermath, this show-down between the monarchy and the realm's most powerful baronial family had major repercussions. One effect was that it provided the combatants with a theatre of war in which to experiment with the new-fangled weapon.

The final act in the drama unfolded at Threave Castle in the summer of 1455. By the time of James II's arrival at the siege in early July, all the other Douglas strongholds – from Lochindorb in the north to Douglas itself – had fallen, thanks largely to the king's artillery. These included 'the gret gun the quhilk a Frenchman schot richt wele' at the siege of Abercorn. This may have been the same 'great bombard' that was hauled in June, at great expense and no little inconvenience, from Linlithgow Palace to Threave; it was emphatically not Mons Meg for, contrary to local tradition,

she did not arrive in the country until two years later. The siege dragged on for two months, during which time James, the ninth and last earl of Black Douglas, fled to England and entrusted his island fastness into the custody of the English king, Henry VI. King James, despairing of ever taking the castle by storm, was forced into bribing the garrison into surrendering.

The most likely explanation for the king's failure to wrest Threave Castle by force was the presence of the formidable artillery fortification that had been wrapped around the fourteenth-century tower house prior to the siege (see **36**). This structure, described as the 'artillery house' in 1458, was a most remarkable construction, without parallel anywhere else. It took the form of two stone walls, 5m (16ft) high, built at 90

60 The box-machicolation projecting from the front wall of Lochranza Castle, Arran. This simple device enabled the defenders to protect the entrance door below.

degrees to each other. Three circular gun towers, one at the point where the two walls met and the others at either end, projected out into the surrounding water-filled ditch. A gateway protected by a drawbridge was built mid-way along one wall. The lengths of wall were battered, or sloped, externally in an attempt to reduce the impact of incoming gunstones, and provided with vertical slits, for use presumably by archers armed with crossbows and longbows. There is evidence for a wall-walk accessed from timber staging. The gun towers were three-storeyed, the lower two storeys fitted with three gunholes each, some shaped like a dumb-bell and some like an inverted keyhole. The top level was open to the elements and provided with a more conventional crenellated parapet (**61**).

In the early days of the siege, the earl of Douglas was accused of treason by king and parliament for fortifying and arming his castle of Threave. That they were compelled to act in this way because of the construction of this extraordinary artillery fortification received startling confirmation during excavations on the island in the 1970s. These showed that the two high-status buildings erected for Archibald 'the Grim' in front of his tower house had been demolished by the later fifteenth century, presumably to provide a clear field of fire for the gunners within the new fortification (see **36**). One of the gun towers also had an occupation level dated to the late fifteenth century. Moreover, a precise date of 1447 for the construction of the less substantial artillery wall along the river side came from the tree-ring dating of the timber carrying the harbour gate. At this date William, the eighth earl, was still alive and the process of strengthening the island fastness against possible aggression seems to have been initiated by him. Following his murder at the king's own hand at Stirling Castle in 1452, the struggle was continued by his younger brother, James, the ninth earl. Clearly, the confrontation between Stewart and Douglas had been brewing for some considerable time.

Guns and gunholes

The precise nature of the guns the Douglases planned to poke through Threave's gunholes is not clear, though given the diameter of the apertures, 280mm (11in), they were clearly not bombards (Mons Meg had a muzzle 500mm (20in) across). A forged iron breech-loader, with a detachable chamber to hold the gunpowder charge, has been suggested. The barrel would have been bound to a wooden stock, which probably had a swivel-pin in its underside for fitting into a timber sill. Square holes in the sides of some of Threave's gunholes housed such sills. The numerous gunstones found in the harbour at Threave point to guns with calibres of 65 and 80mm (2½ and 3in), of a type known as 'serpentine'.

The Douglases' innovative free-standing artillery fortification, intended chiefly for use by guns against guns, was not followed in Scotland for another fifty years. The more usual approach was rather more conservative, simply providing castle walls with gunholes at strategic points. Even then, the number of castles so improved appears to have been quite small. The gunholes followed the two forms employed at Threave, with the 'inverted keyhole' type the more popular. Cardoness, not far from Threave Island, had four incorporated into its ground floor. The gatehouse into George Maxwell's Newark Castle (Renfrewshire) was given both types (**62**), although interestingly the tower house itself was given none, the traditional simple slits deemed sufficient by the laird. By the end of the century a third form had joined them, the 'crosslet keyhole' type, though given its restricted distribution in the north-east (at Ravenscraig in Aberdeenshire, and Arbuthnott and Glenbervie, both Kincardineshire) it was clearly just a regional variant.

There are two other castles, though, which appear to have had substantial artillery works carried out on them during the century, Craigmillar and Ravenscraig (Fife). The inner curtain wall with its four gun-looped projecting towers, wrapped around the early fifteenth-century L-plan tower house at Craigmillar, has already been mentioned on account of its splendid machicolated wall-head (see **59**). This feature, and an eighteenth-century reading of the date 1427 below the armorial over the entrance doorway, have previously led to the dating of the curtain wall to the first half of the century. Recently that date has been called into question and a date in the early sixteenth century proposed, though the reasoning seems rather unconvincing. The towered curtain with its high, crenellated walls, however, has a very traditional 'medieval' feel about it, far more than Threave's innovative design, and it also served to provide extra castle

61 An impression of the central gun tower at Threave Castle in use during the 1455 siege. Drawn by David Simon.

62 The gatehouse into Lord Maxwell's castle at Newark Castle, Port Glasgow, Renfrewshire, built about 1480. The structure was fitted with two forms of gunhole, a 'dumbell' (to the left of the arched entry and pointing into the field) and an 'inverted keyhole' (to the right and covering the adjacent barmkin wall, now gone).

accommodation. A date in the second quarter of the century seems perfectly acceptable. Given that gunholed structures were already well established elsewhere by 1400 (for example, in England at Bodiam Castle, Sussex, and in France at Blanquefort Castle), and given the date of Threave, there is no justification, on present evidence, for dating Craigmillar to a century later.

There is, though, more justification for calling into question the 1460–3 date for the works carried out at Ravenscraig but ordered by James II before his tragic death in 1460 (63). It used to be thought that when that building programme was brought to a premature conclusion in 1463 the new castle consisted of the two end towers but only the lower half of the central range. These parts incorporated keyhole gunholes. When the upper part of the central range was completed, to serve as a gun-platform rather than as a great hall as had originally been intended, wide-mouthed gunholes were inserted, indicating a date in the sixteenth century. A recent study of the masons' marks, however, strongly suggests that the only parts completed by 1463 were the east tower and the foundations of the central range, and the only keyhole gunhole there is clearly a later insertion. The rest of the ground floor of the central range and the whole of the west tower were built in a second phase, conceivably after the Sinclair earls of Orkney took possession of the castle after 1470. This might represent a mere decade of a difference, but it alters significantly our perception of Ravenscraig as a purpose-built artillery fortification.

The loss of Berwick and the defence of the realm

It has been argued that the fortifications at Ravenscraig were part of a wider scheme designed to improve the coastal defences around

66 The caponier in the great ditch at Craignethan Castle, near Crossford, Lanarkshire, as excavated in 1964.

defensive threat, and Finnart rose splendidly to the challenge. There he created a fortification of revolutionary form and incredible strength. It consisted chiefly of a 5m (16ft) thick stone rampart built across the spur. Sadly, the slighting of the castle in 1579 resulted in its demolition and we now have no way of determining either its full height or its detailed appearance. The reconstruction drawing attempts to convey an impression of its undoubted former grandeur; vaulted casemates for trestle-mounted guns at ground level, and a broad, crenellated parapet at the top for heavier, carriage-mounted cannon (**colour plate 13**). The great, flat-bottomed ditch fronting the rampart does still exist, though it was only rediscovered 30 years ago, and in the bottom of that ditch was found Craignethan's most remarkable feature.

The caponier discovered in 1962 was a stone-vaulted, gunholed gallery from within which soldiers armed with handguns could scour the ditch (**66**). The name derived from the Italian *capannata*, meaning 'little hut', and the prototype was apparently invented in Italy, by Francesco di Giorgio Martini, about 1500. Caponiers had a very limited life at the time, and the only other sixteenth-century caponier surviving in Britain is, not surprisingly, at Blackness. The problem seems to have been the lack of ventilation in the cramped vault, for no sooner did the gunners fire off a volley than they were suffocated by gunpowder smoke (**67**).

Angle-bastioned fortifications

The Dunbar blockhouse and Craignethan's west rampart certainly represented a new departure in artillery fortification for Scotland, and yet both were already outmoded when compared with military engineering on the continent. The

Scottish works, like the Henrician fortresses built along the south coast of England about 1540, were really little more than an extension of the medieval tradition of castle fortification. But such works were already a thing of the past in northern Italy where angle-pointed bastions built largely of earth had become the norm for fortresses and town walls alike. Both Finnart and Albany must surely have seen them on their travels, and yet both chose to ignore them.

This is all the more surprising given that the effectiveness of earth as a defence against gunpowdered artillery had already been effectively demonstrated in Scotland. In 1523, Lord Dacre attempted to take Cessford (Roxburghshire), the impressive mid-fifteenth-

century tower-house castle of Sir Andrew Ker, warden of the East March. Armed to the teeth with three heavy siege guns and eight lighter pieces, Dacre's men spent a whole day toiling without success to seize the place. Dacre's explanation for his failure to take it by force was that the castle was 'vawmewred with earth of the best sort I have seen'; a 'vawmure' being an earthwork raised against a wall-face.

The first hint of the use in Scotland of the earthen, angle-pointed bastion – *trace italienne* as it has become known – comes in the 1540s from Edinburgh Castle. Following the English invasion of 1544, a major scheme of refortification was put in hand there which included the construction of an angular earthwork, later called the Spur, projecting out over Castle Hill, under where the eighteenth-century Esplanade now lies. The engineer responsible may have been the

67 An impression of the Craignethan caponier in use in 1540, drawn by Harry Bland.

Italian, Migliorino Ubaldini, sent to Scotland by Henri II of France, the future father-in-law of Queen Mary.

It was following a further invasion in September 1547 that the English themselves began to take a closer interest in *trace italienne* fortification to defend the new garrisons which the duke of Somerset was counting on to consolidate his hold on the country. They had already dabbled in the form, and learnt much through their defence of Boulogne, and in the spring of that year had constructed a modest angle-bastioned work on the Isle of Wight. But it was Scotland that provided the theatre of war in which to test and further perfect the new breed of fortification.

Between Somerset's breathtaking victory over the Scottish host at Pinkie in 1547 and the signing of the Treaty of Boulogne in March 1550, by which the English were forced out of 'the boundis of Scotland', the English erected six major garrison fortresses, reaching from Roxburgh on the Border, to Broughty on the Firth of Tay, and as far inland as Lauder, in the shadow of the Lammermuir Hills. The others were at Eyemouth on the Berwickshire coast a little to the north of Berwick-upon-Tweed, and at Dunglass and Haddington, both in East Lothian. Alas, nothing survives today of the mightiest of them, Haddington, and scarcely anything of Broughty or Lauder. Only at Dunglass, Roxburgh and Eyemouth are there now significant remains.

All shared the same technique of fortification. The basic principle was a reliance on enormously thick earthen ramparts, which would soak up the incoming artillery shot, augmented by arrowhead-shaped bastions projecting into the field. A careful attention to geometry ensured that every face, whether on bastion or rampart, was 'covered' by another part of the fortification. Stone was hardly used, being restricted to the outer faces of the ramparts and bastions and the bases of the gun-platforms, as excavations at Eyemouth recently showed.

Eyemouth and the beginnings of *trace italienne* in Britain

Eyemouth was the first fort to be built, over the winter of 1547–8; this was one of the attractions of *trace italienne* works, they were quick, and comparatively inexpensive, to build (**68**). Sir Richard Lee's design centred on a single bastion midway along a 15m (50ft) thick rampart cutting off the promontory. Gun-flankers behind the bastion protected the two faces of the rampart, and a broad, flat-bottomed ditch ran in front of all. The bastioned rampart, armed by late 1549 with about ten guns, protected a garrison which was never large, the normal complement consisting of the captain, several lieutenants, a master gunner, two porters, a drummer, a surgeon, an ensign and a clerk plus ten light-horsemen and thirty-four hackbutters.

There was one significant flaw in Lee's original design; the faces of the bastion were not 'covered' by flanking fire from the rampart. These 'blind spots' were only overcome by inserting gun-emplacements in the rampart, thereby weakening the rampart itself. Why Lee opted for a single, central bastion, rather than two bastions, one at each end of the rampart, which would have solved the problem, can only be put down to his incomplete grasp of the principles of the new fortification. Interestingly, when the French reoccupied the fortress in 1557, they abandoned Lee's earlier defence and built just that, a rampart with two terminal angle-bastions further towards the land.

In the event, the English fortresses failed to advance Edward VI's cause, just as the great peels built for his namesake two centuries earlier had failed. But none of Somerset's fortresses was found wanting when put to the test; not even the full might of the Franco-Scottish alliance could dislodge the English from their greatest achievement, Haddington. They might have been short-lived affairs, but the lessons learnt were long lasting. Sir Richard Lee went on to create the mighty fortifications we see today at Berwick-upon-Tweed, and over a century later another 'protector', Oliver

68 Eyemouth Fort, Berwickshire, from the north-east. Lee's arrow-headed bastioned rampart, built in 1547–8, is clearly visible cutting off the narrowest part of the neck of the promontory. Less distinct is the rampart constructed by the French in 1557 beyond Lee's work (that is, towards where the caravan park is now). This had a bastion at either end. The garrison buildings of both forces lay on the grassy headland itself.

Cromwell, looked to angle-bastioned forts to help him achieve his goal. And just as Scotland lays claim to having in Eyemouth the first Italianate fortress built in Great Britain, so it can also boast of having the best in Fort George (Inverness-shire), the mighty garrison fortress built in the aftermath of Culloden, the battle fought on a windswept moor close by in 1746.

(*Fortress Scotland and the Jacobites*, a companion volume in this series, examines these later military structures.)

Castles and cannon

Blockhouses, gun towers, caponiers and angle bastions, for exclusive use by gunners, were confined to royal castles, coastal defences and garrison fortresses. Only Craignethan was exceptional, just like its creator, for no other lordly residence of the sixteenth century, other than Tantallon, included an artillery fortification *per se* in its construction. But the majority of castles built from the 1560s onwards incorporated horizontal gunholes of one form or another somewhere in their walls.

As a rule, these could be counted on the fingers of one hand, and might be randomly scattered about the building. Most were located on the ground floor, often positioned close to an entrance. Exceptionally, they were placed higher up; high in the west gable of Smailholm Tower is a gunhole, inserted in the 1540s, which has its sill scooped out to allow the gunner to rake the barmkin entrance below. Their design also varied: as well as the round-ended type found at Dunbar, there were plain rectangular ones, ones with stepped outer splays to stop bullets from ricocheting into the throat, and some very fancy ones. Towards the end of the century, smaller gunholes placed beneath the sills of upper-floor windows started to appear (**69**), as well as little shot-holes, for use with pistols.

Most gunholes were intended to be used to ward off undesirable intruders – as William Forbes, of Corse Castle (Aberdeenshire), allegedly vowed in 1581: 'I will build me such a house as thieves will need to knock at ere they enter.' They were certainly not capable of withstanding a more determined attack. As with most other aspects of castle design, their appearance was probably as much to do with aesthetic considerations as defensive ones. The attractive triplet-gunholes adorning the gatehouse facade of William Forbes' seat at Tolquhon Castle (Aberdeenshire), built in the 1580s, can only have been for show; there was no way they could practically be used with the guns he had founded at the same time (**70**). And the little shot-holes visible on the outside of the turrets at Fairnilee (Selkirkshire), a seat of the Ker family built about 1600, do not even penetrate through to the inside!

St Andrews – a castle under siege

Most castles and fortified homes, if they were subjected to attack at all, would have witnessed only lightly armed assaults. Only the major royal and baronial castles were subjected to more fully pressed sieges, such as at Tantallon in 1528, and then only occasionally. One of the

69 Children fill in their worksheets at a gunholed window in the late sixteenth-century Ruthven Lodging at Dirleton Castle. The gunhole was intended to deter intruders, and the window was also once fitted with an iron cage grille and bars (see the holes in the stonework) for the same reason.

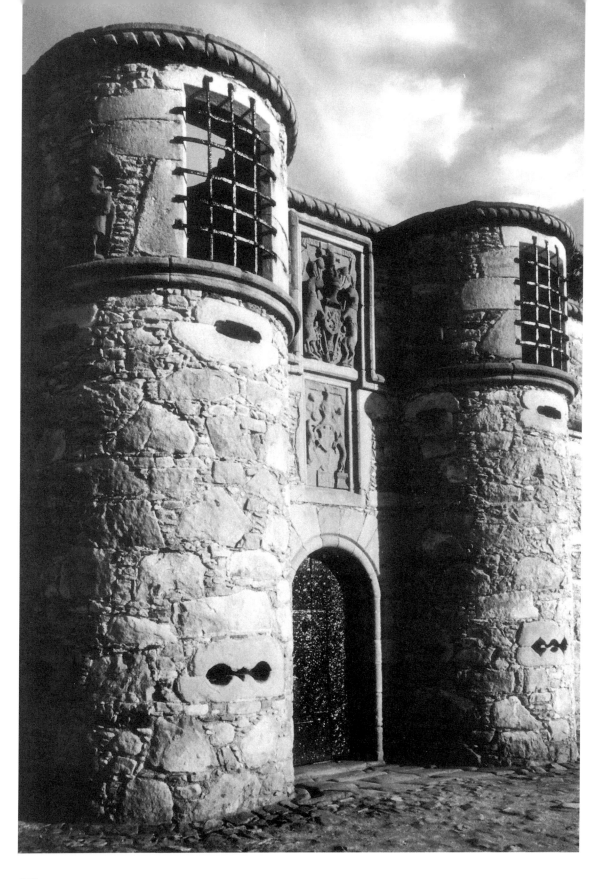

70 William Forbes' attractive gatehouse at Tolquhon Castle, near Tarves, Aberdeenshire, with its fancy gunholes, grilled windows, sculptured figures and armorial panels. The gatehouse was surely designed more to impress than to deter.

most bitterly contested was the assault on St Andrews Castle of 1546–7 which dragged on for fourteen months. That siege has left evidence of itself in one of the most interesting pieces of siege engineering to survive anywhere in Europe – the mine and countermine (71).

The siege began in May 1546 following the assassination of its lord, Cardinal Beaton (72), and the occupation of the castle by his assassins, a group of Fife lairds and Protestant sympathizers. By this date the episcopal residence was a formidable stronghold, for not only were the two flanking gun-towers mentioned on page 102 in place but the cardinal himself had carried out further strengthening works, chiefly the substantial thickening of the frontal wall. These works contrived to thwart

Regent Arran's attempts to take the place by artillery bombardment; other measures were required.

In November the French ambassador in London reported that Arran's men were digging a mine beneath the castle walls in an attempt to force an entry. To forestall them, he noted, the defenders were counter-mining. The fruits of their endeavours, filled in immediately after the siege ended, were rediscovered in 1879 and are there for all to see (73). The mine was a spacious stepped corridor, high and wide enough for pack animals to be used in it to remove the rock more speedily. Surprisingly, the entrance to the mine was situated within 40m (130ft) of the castle walls, demonstrating just how close-fought medieval siege warfare was.

The countermine, by contrast, was a cramped affair, testifying to the desperation of the

71 Drawing showing the location of the mine and countermine at St Andrews Castle, Fife.

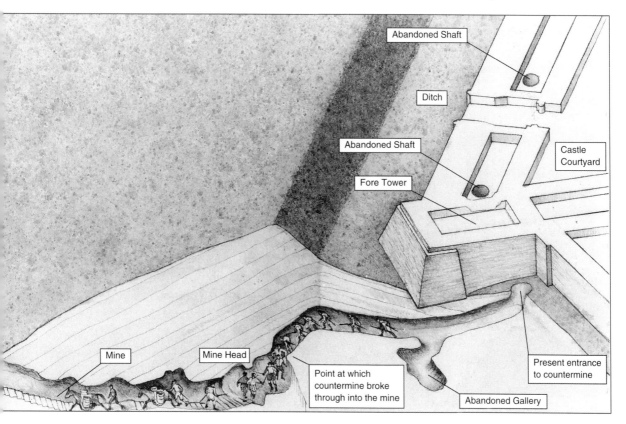

Abandoned Shaft

Ditch

Abandoned Shaft

Fore Tower

Castle Courtyard

Mine

Mine Head

Point at which countermine broke through into the mine

Present entrance to countermine

Abandoned Gallery

72 Cardinal David Beaton; a painting on display in the Abbot's Hall, Arbroath Abbey. The monastery was one of the cleric's several benefices.

folk, with the exception perhaps of those on the English Border, life generally would have been reasonably peaceful, interrupted only now and then by the noise of unfriendly voices and the sound of guns. The castles built during the century are testimony to this.

In the 1509 charter granted to John Grant, binding him to carry out defensive works to Urquhart, is an outline also of the kind of residence he was expected to build. He was 'to construct within the castle a hall, chamber, and kitchen, with all the requisite offices, such as pantry, bakehouse, brewhouse, oxhouse, kiln, cot, dovegrove, and orchard, with the necessary wooden fences'. This conjures up in the mind's

defenders, who by now included John Knox, the fiery Protestant preacher. In fact, they made two false starts in their attempt to locate the mine before succeeding in breaking through. Eventually, the stout defence was broken only when a heavily armed French force arrived and opened up a murderous artillery bombardment. The castle walls were ripped apart. An eye-witness described the devastation: 'Thate daye thai schote downe all the battellyne and caiphouse of the seytowre; and all this daye tha schate upone the easte parte of the castell ... at the hall and chapell, and dislogid us of that parte be downputting of the ruffis and sklatis.' The proof of that statement is evident in the present remains.

More tall storeys

In the meanwhile, life went on. The horrors of the 1540s might lead us into getting things out of proportion and thinking that castle life during the century was one long round of fighting. In this we would be mistaken. For most

73 The rock-cut mine in St Andrews Castle, dug by the attacking force during the siege of 1546–7.

eye a respectable, and peaceful, country seat, albeit one sheltering behind a stout defence. An inventory of the contents, made in 1545, further adds to our understanding of the castle as residence, with its list of beds, feather beds, bolsters, blankets and sheets, tables, chairs and forms, pots and pans, a chest containing 300 pounds, a brew-cauldron, fire-spits, barrels of oats, and three big boats.

The focal point of John Grant's rebuilt castle was the tall tower house which still dominates the skyline. By now the tower house was the recognized form of lordly residence, adopted at all levels of the landholding class (**colour plate 14**). The new century saw further substantial developments to its layout and detailed design, though it was only with the tower-house boom following the Reformation in 1560 that the most licence was taken.

Edzell Castle – a case study

Typical of the tower-house castles of the first half of the century was Edzell (Angus), the charming residence of the 'lichtsome (carefree) Lindsays' in Glenesk, north of Brechin. It centred on a four-storey L-plan tower house built at one corner of a rectangular courtyard (or barmkin), formed by a defensible wall of middling strength (**74**). The internal arrangement of the tower house followed the pattern of previous centuries, but the entrance into the tower house was now firmly rooted at ground level, where it was 'covered' by a gunhole in the projecting staircase wing. At the wall-top was an attractive parapet rising from a double row of corbels arranged in a chequer pattern – very fashionable throughout the century – with turrets at each angle and in the middle of each length of wall-walk. Beside the tower house stood a rectangular, two-storey range, which incorporated the main entrance into the courtyard at ground level and a suite of rooms on the upper floor (**75**).

The relationship between the tower house and the adjacent range is now impossible to determine. That the two were constructed at different times, the tower house in the 1530s and the extension in 1553, has led to the view that the tower house was very soon perceived as being too cramped and awkward to live in, requiring a more suitably dignified apartment to be built alongside it. This may have been the case, and the fact that for a short time in the middle of the century Edzell came to be held by the head of the Lindsays, the earl of Crawford himself, is one possible reason for the new building.

But there is too the possibility that the tower house and its adjacent range were planned to co-exist from the outset, to form part of an integral unit, but that there was a pause between the two building operations. Bearing in mind the obligations and size of household of the Lindsays, it is certainly very difficult to see the tower house by itself functioning adequately as a noble residence. Possible confirmation that this may have indeed been the case comes from nearby Melgund Castle.

Edzell and Melgund castles compared

Melgund, near Aberlemno (Angus), was built by Cardinal Beaton (see **72**), the cleric murdered in his official residence, St Andrews, in 1546; his arms and initials, together with those of his mistress, Margaret Ogilvie, occur in several places. The appearance of the castle is very like Edzell's, a tall tower house with a two-storey range attached. But whereas Edzell's development is clearly a staged affair, as the risband (vertical) joints in the outer walls clearly show, Melgund was built all of one piece, a fact recently confirmed by an analysis of the many masons' marks in the fabric.

The distribution of those marks offers a nice insight into how building works might have progressed. Construction work seems to have begun with the tower house, for some of the masons who worked on the ground floor of the hall block only joined the job once the tower house was up to first-floor level. Thereafter, work continued simultaneously on the upper part of the tower house and the central part of

74 The L-plan tower house in Edzell Castle, Angus, built in
the 1530s by the Lindsays as their private residence.

75 An impression of the entrance front of Edzell Castle as it might have looked in 1600. The earliest part is the L-plan tower house (about 1530) at the right end. The central range, containing the entrance at ground level and a great hall over, was built about 1553, and the gable and round tower at the left end towards the end of the century. Drawn by David Simon.

the hall block, before the masons moved on to complete the rest of the hall block furthest from the tower house.

The arrangement of the accommodation is more clear at Melgund than at Edzell (76). It comprised the lord's private lodging in the tower house, a great hall in the centre of the adjacent range with a withdrawing room at the far end. The architect of Melgund, therefore, managed to create a fully integrated lordly residence where the public and private elements were brought together under the one roof. Edzell, which

shared some of the Melgund masons, seems to have achieved that only in stages. A plausible conclusion, from a study of the masons' marks, is that Edzell's tower house was completed in its entirety in the late 1530s, at which point the masons moved to Melgund, where they carried through the whole project, before returning once more to Edzell to complete the hall block in 1553. That would suggest that Melgund was completed within ten years.

Beaton's baronial household

Cardinal Beaton built Melgund not for himself but for his eldest natural son, David. The cardinal himself resided elsewhere in a number of residences, including the abbot's house at Arbroath Abbey, the bishop's castle in St Andrews (following his elevation to the archbishopric of St Andrews in 1539), on the episcopal manor at Monimail, also in Fife, and

113

76 An impression of the arrangement of the main accommodation in Melgund Castle, near Aberlemno, Angus. Drawn by David Simon.

in his lodgings in Edinburgh, at the corner of Blackfriars' Wynd and Cowgate. By the time he succeeded his uncle, James Beaton, as primate of Scotland, he was already at the pinnacle of his career, ruling 'a kingdom within a kingdom', and his household was that of a great nobleman. Wherever his grace was, there was his household, or a considerable part of it, attending to all his needs, both professional and personal. The numbers might not have been quite as large as those serving a great thirteenth-century magnate, like Walter Moray of Bothwell, but they would still have been formidable, and they all required to be housed somewhere.

Beaton's household consisted on the one hand of his professional *familia*, his group of experienced administrators, secretaries and clerks, and on the other of his personal officials and servants. The former were largely composed of relatives and friends from his upbringing in the East Neuk of Fife. They were all people whom he could trust, like George Durie, his cousin, abbot of Dunfermline and archdeacon of St Andrews, who was scarcely out of his company and the most frequent witness of his master's writs; and Bernard Bailie, a distant relation, parson of Lamington, in Clydesdale, who became his closest friend and curator of the young laird of Melgund. They spent much of their time in their master's company, but they had their own residences to which they would have retired from time to time.

His personal staff, though, would have been permanently bound to their master's side. The most trusted was John Beaton of Balfour, his nephew, who was captain of St Andrews Castle;

under him were the small army of guards, men-at-arms and gunners (77). Then there was his private writing office, headed by another nephew, John Lauder, and his colleague, Andrew Oliphant, Beaton's 'weel belovit clerk'; his two chaplains, who looked after his private chapel, and two almoners, who looked after the needy at the castle gate (see, for example, 40); his master of works, who had charge of the masons, barrowmen, smiths and wrights working on refortifying the castle during much of the cardinal's episcopacy; his provisor, who victualled the castle with food and drink; the master of his household, with his 'army' of cooks and kitchen staff, including the keeper of the pewter; the master of the horse and his stable hands; the minstrels, upholsterers, baker, brewer and gardeners and a host of personal attendants, pages, lackeys, tailors, barber and apothecary. As if that wasn't enough, there were about another twenty assorted servants, including his fool. Other than the 'high heid yins', many of the lower-ranking servants remain nameless in the records, but we do know that the unfortunate castle porter, killed on the same day as his master, was Ambrose Stirling, and that Gabriel, the cook, and Claud, the barber, were French, and that the poor fool went by the name of John Lowys.

Huntly Castle and the noble life

Very little remains now of Cardinal Beaton's residence in St Andrews Castle, it having been so badly damaged during the siege that followed his death that it makes it very difficult for us to envisage how his enormous household was accommodated. We therefore have to look elsewhere, to a castle that has survived relatively complete, which was built about 1550, and by a nobleman of similar standing to Beaton. We have the perfect castle in Huntly (78).

The origins of Huntly Castle go back to the twelfth century, to the time of Earl Duncan of Fife, who built a motte-and-bailey castle in this beautiful setting beside the River Deveron. During the fourteenth century, the castle passed

77 Statue of a crossbowman high up on the south front of the palace in Stirling Castle, built about 1540.

78 Huntly Castle, Aberdeenshire, from the north-east. In the background is the grassy mound of the original motte, built in the later twelfth century, and in the foreground the unfinished early seventeenth-century east range. In the centre, dominating everything, is the palace, the 'new expensive stately building' erected in the mid-sixteenth century by the fourth earl of Huntly, and modified about 1600 by his grandson, the first marquis.

into the hands of the Gordons, a Berwickshire family that had loyally served The Bruce. They were not long in climbing up the social ladder, and by 1449 the head of the house was first earl of Huntly. In 1547, a year after Beaton's murder, George Gordon, the fourth earl, was appointed lord chancellor of Scotland, and his elevation to one of the highest offices of State prompted him to erect a 'new expensive stately building, which he had joined to the old castle and rendered a very convenient place'. The new residence was ready in time for the visit in 1556 of Mary of Guise, now the queen-regent.

The reception Mary received was magnificent. She was welcomed at the castle gates by a guard of honour of 1,000 men, and the splendour of her entertainment was such that, after a few days, she wished to depart so as to relieve the burden on her host. Huntly assured her that his cheer was within his means and astonished her by displaying the spacious vaults crammed with provisions. Those vaults survive yet, as does much of the rest of the earl's residence, and despite the alterations that were subsequently made to the place, it is perfectly possible to picture it at the time of the queen's visit.

The 'old castle' mentioned above was the L-plan tower house that now exists as foundations only; it was blown up during a siege by James VI in 1594. Little more can be said about it except that it was probably built about 1400, to serve as the lordly apartment within the castle, but that by the time of the royal visit, had been downgraded to provide accommodation for senior members of the earl's household and their servants.

The earl's residence was now relocated in the 'new expensive stately building', known today

as the palace. It was oblong on plan with a large round tower projecting from one corner (**79**). It has been argued that such projecting towers, whether round or square, were built primarily for defensive reasons, to 'cover' adjacent walls (there were similar round towers added at Edzell and Melgund), and the existence of two wide-mouthed gunholes in the tower at Huntly gives some credence to this. But I cannot help but feel that the motivation had more to do with attractiveness than earnestness, and even today, in its ruined state, the mighty round tower is powerfully impressive.

The lowest of the five storeys was given over to three storage cellars in the main block and a grim prison in the basement of the round tower. On the first floor in the main block was a kitchen flanked by two cellars, conceivably the pantry (from the French *paneterie*, bread store) and buttery, or wine cellar (from the French *bouteillerie*, bottle store), and in the tower, above the prison, a room which was probably the steward's chamber, for it was well lit, had a fireplace and a latrine closet, and, crucially, had two back-stairs giving access to the earl's suite of rooms on the floor above.

The earl's apartment comprised three rooms, two of which are referred to in a document dated 1576. One was called 'the grit chalmer' (great chamber), also referred to as the 'chalmer of daice (dais)', and the other 'his owin chalmer ... quhilk ... was ane round within (that is, beyond) the grit chalmer'. The third room, we may presume, was the earl's hall. This was the conventional arrangement of the day. All three were reception rooms, graded according to the rank of those being received. The hall, the largest in size, was the least restricted of the rooms and served also as dining room; the great chamber was a more intimate room, the ancestor of the drawing room; the inner chamber in the round tower was the earl's bedchamber. Between the great and inner chambers was the earl's latrine closet. The floor above the earl's apartment was identical in plan, with a sequence of three rooms, and was

presumably the countess's suite, for the two leading persons in the castle had separate households. The remainder of the accommodation in the palace is unclear, but the garret may have contained ancillary bedchambers, and there must surely have been a private chapel, perhaps in the range to the east.

We know from an inventory taken after Huntly's fall from grace in 1562 that the palace rooms presented a most impressive picture of wealth and splendour; among the treasures was the silk tent in which Edward II had slept the night before Bannockburn. The rooms themselves had plastered walls draped with tapestries and other embroidered hangings. Most of the floors were covered with woven rush mats, the oriental carpets then becoming fashionable being reserved as ornamental table-covers. Furniture was sparse; apart from the chair and canopy of state in the earl's great chamber, and the richly hung beds, the main pieces were trestle-tables, forms and stools, and chests for storing tableware, linen, furnishings and valuables. A sixteenth-century nobleman's life was still largely peripatetic.

There is one aspect of the noble life which intrigues me: who slept where when the monarch came to stay? Mary of Guise and her entourage must surely have taken precedence over everyone else, including the earl and countess, during her stay in 1556. Did this mean that the earl vacated his apartment in deference to his superior? And if so, did he then displace the countess from her apartment? And if so, whom did she displace? Perhaps it is just as well that there are certain aspects of noble life that we remain ignorant of.

The post-Reformation tower house

The silk tent of Edward II stored at Huntly Castle was part of a treasure-house of riches spirited away from Aberdeen Cathedral in 1559 in anticipation of trouble ahead. It was not long in coming. In the following year, the

Reformation parliament officially recognized the end of Catholicism and the birth of Protestantism as the nation's religion.

This watershed in Scottish history heralded another castle-building boom. But why? The redistribution of Church lands and property into the hands of secular lords after 1560 has traditionally been given as the spur, but in truth this material change had happened a generation and more before 1560, for example with the granting of monastic estates into lay benefices. David Beaton himself effectively held Arbroath Abbey as a private estate after becoming archbishop of St Andrews in 1539.

Perhaps the more likely reason for the building boom was the rising esteem that the lesser lairds, those below the rank of lords of parliament, were attaining during this momentous period of change in Scottish society. Certainly by 1560 they had flexed their muscles to the extent that 100 of them had won the right to sit in the Reformation parliament for the first time, and in its aftermath, these same lairds were to take a much more active role in the organization of the new Church, which was to become more parish based. These 'bonnet lairds' were the ones who contributed most to the new boom.

The plethora of fortified houses, chiefly tower houses, built after 1560 has been contrasted with the comparative dearth of castle building throughout the first half of the century, and the phrase 'the long pause' has been coined to describe this relative barrenness. However, we need to be more cautious about depicting the period up to the Reformation as a half-century of dearth in castle construction. We have seen above something of the quality of work underway in Angus between the 1530s and 1550s, and other areas of the country show similar activity. We must also be aware of the possibility that some of the post-Reformation tower houses may simply have been refurbishments of existing buildings.

The lesson of Carsluith Castle (Kirkcudbrightshire) is salutary (**80**). At first sight it looks for all the world like a late

80 The late sixteenth-century L-plan tower house at Carsluith Castle, near Creetown, began life about 1500 as a rectangular building. The projecting jamb was probably added when the new family, the Brouns, took possession in the 1560s and decided to mark their arrival in a very visible way.

sixteenth-century L-plan tower house, and the date in the armorial panel over the front door, now almost illegible but recorded previously as 1568, confirms that view. But a closer inspection of the fabric points to a more complicated building history, for it probably began life as a simple oblong tower built about 1500, in which case the acquisition in 1506 of the lands through marriage by Lindsay of Fairgirth may have been the trigger for the new building. The building operation recorded in the armorial stone seems simply to have been a remodelling of that building by the new owners, the Brouns.

Notwithstanding this caveat, there is no escaping the fact that castle building after 1560 was prodigious. It affected all parts of the country. Furthermore, the architect-masons responsible for the work took the quite simple forms that had been handed down to them to new and exciting heights of planning and design. They explored a multiplicity of ground plans – Ls, Zs, Es and Ts and variants of these; they made improvements to the quality of life inside the tower; and they exercised considerable ingenuity in the treatment of the exteriors, particularly the wall-head.

Claypotts – the residence of a bonnet laird

One point worth bearing in mind when looking at the post-Reformation tower house is the likely status of the builder. Normally, a bonnet laird had just one modest estate, with equally modest obligations to go with it. The size of his household was tailored to these needs, and so was his residence. Claypotts, the home near Dundee of the Strachans, is typical of these residences of bonnet lairds (**colour plate 15**).

At the beginning of the sixteenth century, the Strachans were lay tenants in Claypotts, holding the land of the abbey of Lindores. They also held other small farms nearby from the abbeys of Arbroath and Balmerino. For their principal holding, Claypotts, they paid the abbot a £12 annual rent with twelve cockerels thrown in for good measure. In addition, they were liable to attend the monastic court when required, and in time of war were obliged to provide a quarter of the cost of an armed horseman with an attendant foot soldier. This situation continued up to the Reformation, when the unfortunate monks of Lindores had to endure the sight of their church being wrecked by the Reformers. But, in common with many of their monastic brethren, they were allowed to remain in their cloister for the rest of their days so long as they embraced the new faith – which they did.

The new relationship between John Strachan and the abbot of Lindores spurred the former to embark on a new building, to reflect his new-found status. Within a decade of the Reformation parliament, work had begun on constructing the present building of Claypotts; the date 1569 is carved on the fabric. It took twenty years to complete. The tower house was built on the Z-plan, with two round towers projecting from diametrically opposed corners of the main block. Whether this was for reasons of defence or show cannot now be determined. There is no doubting the earnestness of the twelve wide-mouthed gunholes at ground level, or the defensive capability of the two barriers at the entrance, but these features, and others we find on buildings of this date – like iron grilles over windows (see **69** and **70**) and timber drawbars behind doors and window shutters (**81**) are the late-medieval equivalents of today's outside security lights, door-chains and window locks. The Strachans of this world were just as concerned as us about intruders.

The internal arrangements at Claypotts were broadly similar to those in earlier tower houses, but with important differences. Two stairs were now provided – the main (public) stair and the back (service) stair – so that the gentle folk of the house would not have to rub shoulders with the servants. The sanitary arrangements were also improved, for the draughty open-chuted latrine was now replaced by portable soil boxes (something like the modern chemical toilet) which could be emptied as required. The kitchen

81 A timber drawbar recently discovered in a ground-floor window at Ballencrieff Castle, near Aberlady, East Lothian.

was also now an ever-present feature. Hitherto, many tower houses had been without a formal kitchen, because the main room for dining in was the great hall, situated elsewhere in the castle complex. Any cooking done in the tower house would have been done informally over the hall fire (see **47**). But bonnet lairds did not have the substantial obligations of the senior nobility, like Beaton and Huntly, and so did not need such complex residences. For the first time in the long history of the Scottish castle, we can say of these modest later sixteenth-century tower houses that they were the 'be all and end all' of the lairdly residence, more akin to a private home than a public place of lordship (**82**).

Just in case we are in any doubt as to the relative standing of John Strachan and his like to the Beatons and the Huntlys of that time, a

peep into his last will and testament, drawn up in 1593, confirms his modest standing. Three women looked after his house, including Janet Wilkie who had been with the family for fourteen years. Four ploughmen and a shepherd worked his land, and in that year they had 'sawin on the ground of Claypotts' 8 bolls of wheat, 50 bolls of oats, 14 bolls of barley and 6 bolls of peas, and tended 79 sheep, 14 oxen, 7 bullocks, 5 cows and 2 workhorses. Add to all this the value of his 'guidis, geir, sowmes of money and dettis perteining' and we have a bonnet laird worth £1,222 6s. 8d. at his death. This put John Strachan a cut above the average farmer or small laird, who was worth little more than £500 at that date. Claypotts Castle was therefore the residence of a farmer of above average means – and it shows.

If Claypotts was at the top end of the scale of residences built by 'bonnet lairds', then Fourmerkland Tower, north of Dumfries, was pretty well near the bottom. Built about 1590

82 An impression of John Strachan's hall on the first floor in Claypotts Castle, Broughty Ferry, as it might have looked in 1590. Drawn by David Simon.

by Robert Maxwell, a relation of the earl of Herries, it was one of the smallest post-Reformation tower houses, with a floor area totalling no more than 70sq m (750sq ft), a third of the size of Claypotts. But everything is relative, and although his modest fortified house may pale into insignificance alongside Claypotts, in terms of his standing in Border society Robert Maxwell was among the top 5 per cent of landholders in terms of wealth, with an estate valued at £300 at his death. There were many other small-time lairds below him, and their fortified homes reflected this.

Fortified farm houses on the Border and beyond

In the lonely valley of the Jed Water, 8km (5 miles) south of Jedburgh and within sight of England, stands the isolated ruin known as Slacks Tower (83). Surrounded today by crumbling stone dykes and grazing sheep, Slacks in the late sixteenth century was the throbbing heart of a small farm held by one of the Oliver 'surname', a noted reiving family. William Oliver 'of Slakis' took part in a raid in 1583.

The ruin still stands pretty well to roof height and the arrangement of the

83 Slacks Tower, south of Jedburgh, Roxburghshire, from the north-east, with the remains of farm buildings around it. The two upper floors, comprising the main accommodation, were entered through a first-floor door in the side wall (where the gap is). The ground floor was separately accessed through a door in the right-hand gable.

accommodation is clear enough. The building consisted of three floors including a garret, all unvaulted. The ground floor was entered separately through a doorway in the downward-facing gable, originally fitted with two doors, one presumably of timber opening outwards, and the other, an iron yett, opening inwards and further strengthened by a timber drawbar. A second doorway in a side wall, reached from the ground by an outside timber stair, gave access to the upper floors; it was similarly defended. The upper floors had small windows, which is more than the ground floor had, and the main floor was heated from an open hearth with a smoke-hood, or 'hingin' lum', above it. Access to the garret must have been by ladder. Even though the amount of living space (100sq m/1,076sq ft), is greater than that at Fourmerkland, all in all, the impression is of a rude lairdly dwelling.

84 Plan of Slacks farm.

It has been said of buildings like Slacks that they were temporary shelters in times of trouble, bolt-holes where their owners, their servants, tenants and possessions could shelter whenever a cross-border raid or internal feud threatened. Normal daily life was lived in the less substantial dwellings of timber and turf placed around the building, and these survive, albeit as foundations only, remarkably well at Slacks (84). But I find this picture very hard to credit.

There is no gainsaying the fact that structures like Slacks were used to shelter people and possessions, including livestock, at critical times (eight cattle were burnt to death inside William Douglas's farm house at Cunzierton (Dumfriesshire) during a raid in 1540), but this does not preclude them from being used as permanent residences. Would Border lairds like the Olivers really have left the best building on their farm unoccupied for a greater part of the time? I doubt it.

There is no getting away from the fact that life on both sides of the Border in the years either side of 1600 was particularly troubled. Reiving and feuding were endemic, law and order conspicuously absent. For families like the Olivers security was uppermost in their minds. But they would only have built robust buildings like Slacks if they had something worth protecting. When we look on Slacks today, lonely and slowly crumbling before our eyes, it is only too easy to conjure up a picture of a scruffy reiver mucking out the byre by day and raiding over the Border by night. But the truth is that the Olivers and their like had never been wealthier. No matter how they had come by that wealth – and the Olivers took as much as

85 Glenochar bastel-house, in the Lowther Hills, Lanarkshire. Unlike Slacks Tower, this building had a stone-vaulted ground floor and an internal stair leading to the upper level. Like Slacks, it is surrounded by numerous other buildings.

they lost, like any reivers worth their salt – the fact remains that they were comparatively well off and wished to stay that way. Their fortified farm houses, like Slacks, were just as much outward and visible signs of wealth and status as the mighty baronial castles and fortified towers of their betters, relatively speaking.

Slacks is one of only a handful of these fortified houses surviving in recognizable condition in the Border country. But they must have been a far commoner sight in their heyday between 1560 and 1650, and field survey is adding examples to the list all the time. Among the most remarkable of recent discoveries is the existence of several buildings, similar in many respects to Slacks, far away from the Border, in Upper Clydesdale. Some have been found hiding inside later structures, while others have been discovered lurking in remote valleys in the wilds of the Lowther Hills. Several have been excavated, including those at Glenochar (**85**) and Wintercleuch, both in the parish of Crawford (Lanarkshire). The picture emerging is of structures similar in size to Slacks (that is, with about 100sq m (1,076sq ft) of floor space spread over two floors and a garret) but with differences in the detail, including just the one entrance doorway at ground level, vaulted ground floors with slit openings, and internal stairs. And like Slacks they stand at the hearts of larger complexes comprising less substantial buildings, byres and enclosures.

The discovery of a hoard of coins, including several Elizabethan sixpences, beside the building at Glenochar not only confirms the date of construction and initial occupation but also demonstrates that the laird, whoever he was, was a man of means. So who were the lairds responsible for these Clydesdale examples? Surviving testaments, or wills, clearly show that most were tenant farmers who were becoming wealthier due to their growing flocks of sheep and herds of cattle. Recent research has raised the intriguing possibility that a few may have been associated in some way with the prosperous gold and lead workings in the area. Certainly the lairds at Glendorch (Foulis), Snar (Douglas) and Glengonnar (Bulmer) are known to have been directly involved in the industry. These were men of substance, working 'God's treasure house in Scotland', which, like the Border country, was not without its lawlessness and its share of thieves, murderers and outlaws. The seventeenth century may have dawned, and the king of Scots become the king of England also, but the bonnet lairds of Upper Clydesdale were just as much in need of strong and impressive fortified residences as their predecessors 500 years before.

Epilogue:
a continuing love affair

By any meanes do not take away the battlement ... for that is the grace of the house, and makes it look lyk a castle.

As late as 1689, the Reverend Thomas Morer, an English chaplain serving with a Scottish regiment, wrote: 'The houses of the gentry are high and strong, and appear more like castles than houses, made of thick stone walls, with iron bars for their windows.' His words had a kernel of truth about them, for it took the Scots a long time to cast off their defensive shells. Indeed, in the early years of the century they were even exporting the idea to Ulster as part of the Jacobean 'plantation' (86). And even while Morer was penning his *Short Account*, someone as august as Archibald Douglas, first earl of Forfar, was still residing within the crumbling medieval walls of Bothwell Castle; only as the century drew to its close did he set about building a fine new mansion, Bothwell House, a short distance away. He was not alone. Morer observed this trend: 'Yet now they begin to have better buildings, and to be very modish both in the fabrick and furniture of their dwellings: tho' still their avenues are very indifferent and they want their gardens.'

Even among those building from new during the seventeenth century there were still quite a number, like William 'Danzig Willie' Forbes at Craigievar Castle (Aberdeenshire) and Sir Alexander Nisbet of that Ilk at Nisbet House, near Duns (Berwickshire), who stayed faithful to the lofty, tower-house form. One possible explanation for this conservatism is given in Sir Robert Ker's plea of 1632 to his son, William, regarding the rebuilding of his house at Ancrum, near Jedburgh, quoted above. The age when brave retainers manned the battlements and poured boiling oil on the heads of the besiegers may have passed long since, but crenellations and other castle trappings still served as icons of lordship.

Not that the seventeenth century was all sweetness and light; far from it. James VI, in his dotage, may have boasted: 'This I must say for Scotland, here I sit and govern it with my pen: I write and it is done, and by a clerk of the Council I govern Scotland now, which others could not do by the sword'; but the decades following the Union of the Crowns in 1603 remained troubled ones. Within ten years of Sir Alexander Nisbet building his fortified residence in 1630, and less than three miles away from it on Duns Law, the covenanting army had hastily to erect a bastioned fort from which they could confront Charles I's royalist army; and the earthen ravelins, or gun emplacements, built to protect the likes of Hermitage, Huntly and Tantallon during the civil war that followed, survive to testify to the continuing insecurity. The Cromwellian invasion of 1650 and the subsequent ten-year occupation, and the religious strife that erupted in the 1670s and 1680s continued the uncertainty. Even as late as 1689, during the first Jacobite uprising, castles throughout the Highlands had perforce to become garrisons once more.

86 Monea Castle, Co. Fermanagh, built in 1618 by Malcolm Hamilton, a Lanarkshire gentleman, who settled in Ulster as part of King James VI's plantation and rose to become archbishop of Cashel. With land in excess of 2,000 acres, Hamilton was obliged to build a castle and bawn, the Irish word for a barmkin. The similarity between Monea and Claypotts Castle is striking.

But these were the exception rather than the rule. The mighty castles of medieval magnates were now giving way to magnificent mansions like Drumlanrig Castle (Dumfriesshire), begun about 1676 by the first duke of Queensberry and not really a castle at all. And the tower-house castles of the lesser nobility and gentry were gradually being replaced by more modest lairds' houses – lower, smaller, unvaulted, and only very slightly fortified.

But the Scots have never really ceased their love affair with the castle. They might have let many fall into ruin in the eighteenth century, and

made good use of the stones and slates elsewhere, but somehow these ancient seats of lordship remained as symbols of power. When, in 1715, John Erskine, earl of Mar, plotted his uprising in support of James Stuart, the exiled 'pretender' to the throne of Great Britain and Ireland, it was at his ancestral castle of Kildrummy that he marshalled his forces and from where he embarked on his mission. By the end of the century, ruined castles were becoming compelling features in the landscape; Captain Grose, who sketched so many of them for his *Antiquities of Scotland*, published in 1789, summed up their attraction: 'Let us view the castle of some ancient thane, its hall, its dungeons and embattled towers mantled with ivy.'

This Romantic perception grew and led to a renewed interest in the castle, to the extent that through the nineteenth century a considerable number were repaired to become eye-catching curiosities and the stuff of legend and myth. So

87 Leslie Castle, near Insch, undergoing restoration in 1985.

obsessed were they by the castle that the Scots evolved an architectural style, Scots Baronial, whose debt to the mason-architects of medieval times is patent. And the love affair continues to this day, with some even prepared to invest their life-savings in restoring castles, to serve as useful, and impressive, residences once more.

Perched on haughland beside the Gadie Burn, near Insch in Aberdeenshire, is a lovingly restored castle, Leslie (87). It was one of the last fortified houses built in Scotland, in 1661. But it was very probably also the site of one of the first, for the lands of Lesselyn were acquired in the twelfth century by Bertolf, a Fleming, whose descendants took the name of Leslie. Appropriately, the Leslie family lives there today, and I imagine that they are every bit as proud of their castle as their predecessors.

THE SCOTTISH ROYAL LINE

The Scottish royal line from the eleventh to the seventeenth century, showing in addition relationships with certain other baronial families and also with the English royal succession. Please note that filial relationships are not necessarily shown in the correct order.

Key

D. = Duke
E. = Earl
L. = Lord
m. = married
d. = died

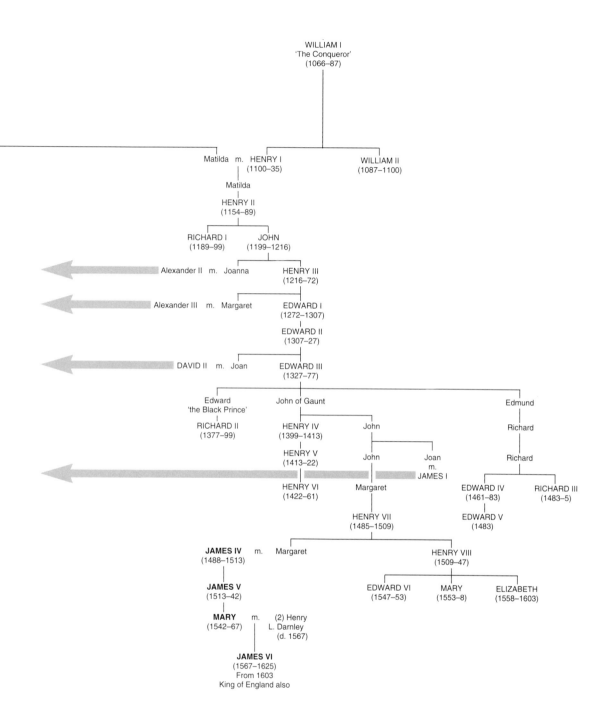

WILLIAM I
'The Conqueror'
(1066–87)

Matilda m. HENRY I
(1100–35)

WILLIAM II
(1087–1100)

Matilda
HENRY II
(1154–89)

RICHARD I
(1189–99)

JOHN
(1199–1216)

Alexander II m. Joanna

HENRY III
(1216–72)

Alexander III m. Margaret

EDWARD I
(1272–1307)

EDWARD II
(1307–27)

DAVID II m. Joan

EDWARD III
(1327–77)

Edward
'the Black Prince'

John of Gaunt

Edmund

RICHARD II
(1377–99)

HENRY IV
(1399–1413)

John

Richard

HENRY V
(1413–22)

John

Joan
m.
JAMES I

Richard

HENRY VI
(1422–61)

Margaret

EDWARD IV
(1461–83)

RICHARD III
(1483–5)

HENRY VII
(1485–1509)

EDWARD V
(1483)

JAMES IV m. Margaret
(1488–1513)

HENRY VIII
(1509–47)

JAMES V
(1513–42)

EDWARD VI
(1547–53)

MARY
(1553–8)

ELIZABETH
(1558–1603)

MARY m. (2) Henry
(1542–67)   L. Darnley
(d. 1567)

JAMES VI
(1567–1625)
From 1603
King of England also

Castles to visit

HS   Historic Scotland
NTS   National Trust for Scotland
LA   Local Authority
P   Private Ownership

Please note that those castles in private ownership are not necessarily readily open to visitors, and permission should be obtained in advance from the owner.

Twelfth-century castles

Aberdour Castle, Fife (HS)
An extensive ruin of the Douglases illustrating how a medieval castle could be extended and modified over several centuries.

Bass of Inverurie, Aberdeenshire (LA)
A fine motte-and-bailey castle built by Earl David of Huntingdon about 1190.

Castle Sween, Argyllshire (HS)
The oldest standing castle in Scotland, built by the MacSweens in the late twelfth century. A substantial pile, only marginally altered in later centuries.

Cubbie Roo's Castle, Orkney (HS)
Probably the earliest stone castle to survive, built about 1145 by the Norseman, Kolbein Hruga. The ruins of a small rectangular tower are enclosed in a circular ditch built over by later structures. Nearby is the ruined twelfth-century St Mary's church.

Duffus Castle, Morayshire (HS)
The finest motte-and-bailey castle in State care, built by Freskin, a Fleming, about 1150. The stone keep on top of the motte and the walls encircling the bailey date from the early fourteenth century.

Edinburgh Castle, Midlothian (HS)
The most famous Scottish castle, with a history of occupation on the castle rock reaching back to the Bronze Age. St Margaret's Chapel (twelfth century), the Fore Well (thirteenth century) and David's Tower (fourteenth century) alone survive from the Middle Ages. The remainder, including the marvellous array of defensive walls, date from the sixteenth century and later.

Huntly Castle, Aberdeenshire (HS)
One of the noblest baronial ruins in Scotland, this castle was the chief residence of the Gordon clan. With a history of occupation extending from the twelfth to the seventeenth century, the complex has a fine motte, the foundations of a large fifteenth-century tower house and, the real wonder, an imposing palace dating from the fifteenth century but substantially remodelled in the mid-sixteenth century and sumptuously enriched about 1600.

Mote of Urr, Kirkcudbrightshire (P)
The finest motte-and-bailey castle in the country, built by Walter de Berkeley about 1160. Excavation showed that the summit was raised in height following the destruction of the timber buildings in the later twelfth century. It is possible that the 'bailey' dates from an earlier period.

Roxburgh Castle, Roxburghshire (P)
The awesome castle mound and encircling ditch are all that survive of this vitally strategic royal castle, built in the early twelfth century at the confluence of the rivers Tweed and Teviot. The chunks of masonry on the summit date from the English occupation after 1296. The outline of the English garrison fort built in the late 1540s can also be made out.

Stirling Castle, Stirlingshire (HS)
A marvellous array of late medieval buildings crowns the summit of the castle rock which overshadows two of the great battlefields in Scottish history – Stirling Bridge in 1297 and Bannockburn in 1314. Pride of place are James IV's great hall and James V's palace.

Thirteenth-century castles

Balvenie Castle, Banffshire (HS)
A curtain-walled castle of the Comyns, remodelled by the Douglases in the fifteenth century, and with a new lodging added by the fourth earl of Atholl about 1550.

Bothwell Castle, Lanarkshire (HS)
One of the outstanding monuments of medieval Scotland, its mighty thirteenth-century donjon is undoubtedly the finest castle fragment surviving in the country. The rebuilding by the Douglases, after the wars with England in the fourteenth century, testifies to their lofty status in society.

Caerlaverock Castle, Dumfriesshire (HS)
Not one but two castles. The older one, built by a Maxwell in the 1220s, was abandoned in the 1270s and replaced by the present castle, one of the most attractive in the country. Besieged by Edward I of England in 1300, it was rebuilt and continued as the Maxwells' chief residence until 1640. The interior has a splendid Renaissance range dating from the 1630s.

Castle Tioram, Argyllshire (P)
A lonely ruin, perched on a rocky island at the head of Loch Moidart, built by the chief of Clan MacRuari. The thirteenth-century curtain wall has fine original features; the tower and other internal buildings date from the fourteenth century and later.

Dirleton Castle, East Lothian (HS)
A formidable fortress built about 1240 for the de Vauxs. Much of their castle survives, despite major refurbishments by the Halyburtons in the later fourteenth century and the Ruthvens in the later sixteenth century.

Drum Castle, Aberdeenshire (NTS)
Built round one of the oldest tower houses in Scotland, this fine castle has a seventeenth-century range and additions by William Burn of 1875.

Duart Castle, Argyllshire (P)
A fine curtain-walled castle of the MacLeans, with a tower house added in the fourteenth century, and other ranges later. The ruin was lovingly restored by Sir Fitzroy MacLean early this century.

Dunstaffnage Castle, Argyllshire (HS)
The impressive curtain-walled castle of the MacDougalls, lords of Lorn, overlooking one of the most important sea-lanes on the western seaboard. Recent excavation suggests that the projecting towers were added later in the thirteenth century. A fine thirteenth-century castle chapel stands close by.

Dunvegan Castle, Skye, Inverness-shire (P)
Ancestral seat of the Clan MacLeod, this is the most famous of all the castles in the Hebrides. In continuous occupation by the same family for over seven centuries, the castle is the longest continuously occupied residence in Scotland. Substantial remains of the medieval curtain-walled castle survive despite the extensive remodelling in Georgian times.

Hailes Castle, East Lothian (HS)
A beautifully-sited ruin by the River Tyne incorporating a thirteenth-century fortified manor. Substantially remodelled by the Hepburns as a tower-house castle from the later fourteenth century, it was a residence of the fourth earl of Bothwell, Mary Queen of Scots' third husband.

Inverlochy Castle, Inverness-shire (HS)
A well-preserved curtain-walled castle of about 1280, built by the Comyns, lords of Lochaber. The largest of the four towers was the donjon, or keep. The place last saw action during the civil war of the 1640s.

Kildrummy Castle, Aberdeenshire (HS)
A substantial ruin of a curtain-walled castle, with projecting towers, great hall and chapel. The gatehouse may be a legacy of Edward I of England. Scene of a great siege in 1306 in which Neil Bruce, Robert the Bruce's brother, was captured.

Lochranza Castle, Arran, Ayrshire (HS)
Entombed within the later medieval tower house are the substantial remains of a hall house.

Peel Ring of Lumphanan, Aberdeenshire (HS)
An earth-and-timber castle, built about 1250 by the Durwards, lords of nearby Coull Castle, possibly as a hunting-lodge. King MacBeth had been killed in the vicinity in 1057.

Rothesay Castle, Buteshire (HS)
A remarkable curtain-walled castle, circular in plan, built by the High Stewart about 1200. Besieged by the Norse in 1230 and again in 1263, it was subsequently strengthened by the addition of four projecting towers. The large forework projecting into the water-filled moat was begun by James IV about 1500.

St Andrews Castle, Fife (HS)
The ruins of the archbishop's residence date from the thirteenth century but the devastating artillery

bombardment during the 1546–7 siege that followed Cardinal Beaton's murder there took its toll. Notable surviving features include the mine and countermine tunnelled during that siege, and the 'bottle dungeon'.

Skipness Castle, Argyllshire (HS)
This modest hall castle of the early thirteenth century was rebuilt as a substantial curtain-walled castle at the end of the century when the Stewart earls of Menteith wrested the place from the MacSween lords of Knapdale. The impressive tower house was added by the Campbells in the early sixteenth century.

Urquhart Castle, Inverness-shire (HS)
A large, sprawling castle majestically sited on the banks of Loch Ness. Originally built by the Durwards, most of the existing ruined buildings, including the lofty tower house, date from after 1509 when the castle was in the hands of the Grants.

Fourteenth-century castles
Doune Castle, Stirlingshire (HS)
Built late in the century for the Regent Albany, but never completed. This large and powerfully impressive courtyard castle has a fine tower house and great hall, restored in the 1880s.

Dundonald Castle, Ayrshire (HS/LA)
The great tower house that dominates the hill was built by Robert II, the first Stewart monarch, about 1370. Excavations have confirmed the existence of a large late thirteenth-century curtain-walled castle and uncovered evidence of occupation reaching back to the Neolithic period.

Hermitage Castle, Roxburghshire (HS)
A vast and eerie ruin in a lonely situation in deepest Liddesdale. Much restored in the nineteenth century, it incorporates elements from the manor house of the Dacres (about 1350) and substantial portions of the unusual tower house built by William, first earl of Douglas. The complex of earthworks has never been excavated and is therefore a mystery. Nearby is Hermitage Chapel, also of the fourteenth century.

Lochleven Castle, Kinrossshire (HS)
Attractively set on an island in the loch, the curtain-walled enclosure is dominated by a rectangular tower house, altered in the sixteenth century and used to imprison Mary Queen of Scots in 1567–8.

Neidpath Castle, Peeblesshire (P)
Dramatically sited beside the River Tweed, this large L-plan tower house was built towards the end of the

century by the Hay family. Much of the interior was remodelled during the sixteenth and seventeenth centuries but there are many fine features from the original building still to be seen.

Tantallon Castle, East Lothian (HS)
A remarkable red sandstone fortress residence perched on a promontory overlooking the North Sea. Built by William, first earl of Douglas, about 1350, it was badly damaged by James V's artillery in 1528 and refortified using green stone. The outworks contain important siege works, including a seventeenth-century ravelin (gun battery).

Threave Castle, Kirkcudbrightshire (HS)
The massive tower house was built by Archibald 'the Grim', lord of Galloway, about 1370, but excavations on the island have shown that this was but the central part of a much bigger complex of buildings. The artillery fortification was built before the great siege of 1455 which saw the downfall of the Black Douglases.

Fifteenth-century castles
Blackness Castle, West Lothian (HS)
Built in the 1440s and massively strengthened by James V in the 1530s as an artillery fortress. Used for much of its life as a state prison and garrison fort.

Borthwick Castle, Midlothian (P)
One of the most impressive tower houses, and certainly one of the largest, it was built by Sir William (later Lord) Borthwick about 1420. Built on the E-plan (without the central stem), it accommodated all the residential and service needs of a nobleman under one roof. The great hall is particularly splendid.

Cardoness Castle, Kirkcudbrightshire (HS)
A well-preserved tower house built by the McCullochs. The outer walls have good, early examples of gunholes, and the interior has high quality carved fireplaces and aumbries.

Castle Campbell, Clackmannanshire (HS)
Formerly called Castle Gloom, this romantically situated castle, flanked by the Burn of Care and the Burn of Sorrow, was adopted by the earls of Argyll as their Lowland seat (their chief seat being at Inveraray, Argyllshire). The fine tower house is complemented by a separate hall block and there are fine seventeenth-century features.

Craigmillar Castle, Midlothian (HS)
The L-plan tower house of about 1400 stood within a curtain wall with a grand machicolated parapet.

The ranges around the courtyard date from the sixteenth and seventeenth centuries. A fishpond in the pleasance, or pleasure garden, to the south of the castle forms the letter P for the Prestons who held the estate for much of its life.

Crichton Castle, Midlothian (HS)
A large and sophisticated castle, originating about 1400 as a tower house and great hall but greatly enlarged to become a courtyard castle by Chancellor Crichton in the 1440s. The most spectacular part, however, is the range erected by Francis Stewart, fifth earl of Bothwell, in the 1580s, which has a most extraordinary Italianate diamond-faceted courtyard facade and the first scale-and-platt stair built in Scotland.

Dean Castle, Ayrshire (LA)
A tower-house castle of the Boyds, added to in the seventeenth century and nicely restored early in the twentieth century. The fifteenth-century tower now houses impressive collections of armour and musical instruments.

Dunnottar Castle, Kincardineshire (P)
The ancestral seat of the Keiths, the earls marischal, and surely one of the most impressively sited castles anywhere. The oldest structure on the promontory is the L-plan tower house of the early fifteenth century; the remainder of the structures are of the later sixteenth and seventeenth centuries. The Honours of Scotland, the country's crown jewels, were hidden here in the 1650s during the Cromwellian interlude.

Huntingtower Castle, Perthshire (HS)
Two fine tower houses, built only 3m (10ft) apart, were eventually incorporated into one grand building in the seventeenth century. The interior contains important sixteenth-century painted walls and ceilings.

Kilchurn Castle, Argyllshire (HS)
A picturesque castle at the head of Loch Awe, built about 1550 by the Campbells of Glenorchy (later earls of Breadalbane). Substantially altered in the 1690s to provide barrack accommodation for the earl's private army.

Kisimul Castle, Barra, Western Isles (P)
The island home of the MacNeils of Barra, consisting of an irregular curtain wall dominated by a tower house. It was restored after the Second World War.

Newark Castle, Renfrewshire (HS)
The tower-house castle of the Maxwells was spectacularly transformed in the 1590s by the wicked Patrick Maxwell into a Renaissance mansion. The fifteenth-century tower house, gatehouse and fragment of barmkin wall survive, as well as impressive interiors from the later mansion.

Orchardton Tower, Kirkcudbrightshire (HS)
A charming little tower-house castle built by the Cairns family. The tower is, uniquely, circular in plan.

Ravenscraig Castle, Fife (HS/LA)
An enigmatic castle, begun by James II shortly before his death in 1460, then continued under the Sinclair earls of Orkney and completed only in the following century. The myth that this was a purpose-built artillery fort must surely be laid to rest. Nevertheless, it has early gunholes of interest.

Rowallan Castle, Ayrshire (HS)
One of the prettiest castles in the country, this residence of the Mures has a ruined fifteenth-century tower house and a roofed sixteenth-century hall block, later altered to form the main residential accommodation. The 'fairytale' twin towers flanking the entrance date from the mid-sixteenth century.

Smailholm Tower, Roxburghshire (HS)
A rectangular tower house and barmkin built by the Pringles, squires of Black Douglas, in the middle of the century. Excavation uncovered an outer hall and chamber to complement the restricted accommodation in the tower, and evidence for a major remodelling by the Scotts (Sir Walter Scott's forebears) after 1640 when the tower was largely replaced by a two-storey house in the courtyard.

Tolquhon Castle, Aberdeenshire (HS)
Built for the Forbes family, Tolquhon has a fifteenth-century tower which was enlarged by William Forbes between 1584 and 1589 with a large mansion round a courtyard. Noted for its highly ornate gatehouse. William Forbes' fine monumental tomb is in the kirkyard in the nearby village of Tarves.

Sixteenth-century castles
Broughty Castle, Angus (HS/Dundee Museums)
A fine tower house, adapted for changing defensive needs during the nineteenth century. Now houses fascinating displays, courtesy of Dundee Museums.

Carnasserie Castle, Argyllshire (HS)
A handsome building, the home of John Carswell, first Protestant bishop of the Isles. The integrated plan of tower house and hall is unusually well preserved, as are the many fine architectural details.

Carsluith Castle, Kirkcudbrightshire (HS)
A pretty ruin of a tower house built in the early part of the century but converted by the Brouns into an L-plan tower after 1560. The flanking ranges are eighteenth-century.

Claypotts Castle, Angus (HS)
A most attractive and complete Z-plan tower house, built in the 1570s for the Strachans. The circular towers on diagonally-opposed corners, corbelled out to form overhanging cap houses, give the building its special charm.

Corgarff Castle, Aberdeenshire (HS)
A rectangular tower house built by the Forbeses, but substantially altered after Culloden into a barracks for 'redcoats'.

Craignethan Castle, Lanarkshire (HS)
A formidable stronghold in an inaccessible situation, typical of its builder, Sir James Hamilton of Finnart. Begun in the 1530s, it was the last noble castle built in Scotland. It was taken by the Crown in 1579 and partly dismantled. The peculiar caponier, or gunners' hut, in the great ditch was discovered during excavation in 1963.

Crathes Castle, Aberdeenshire (NTS)
A lovely L-plan tower house, with notable painted ceilings, dating from the second half of the century. The fine gardens with great yew hedges belong to the early eighteenth century.

Edzell Castle, Angus (HS)
A lovely castle, the property of the 'lichtsome (carefree) Lindsays', with some very important and unique features. The L-plan tower house of about 1530 was soon joined by a hall range. The stunning and fragrant garden, summer house and bath house were added by Sir David Lindsay about 1604.

Elcho Castle, Perthshire (HS)
A handsome and complete tower house, with four projecting towers and some interesting internal features. The original wrought-iron window grilles are still in place, as are some of the timber sills for mounting small guns.

Eyemouth Fort, Berwickshire (LA)
Hugging a promontory overlooking the harbour are the grass-grown remains of the English angle-bastioned garrison fortress built in 1547, and of the French-built fortress that superseded it a decade later.

Glenbuchat Castle, Aberdeenshire (HS)
A fine example of a Z-plan tower house, built by the Gordons in 1590. Its last laird, John Gordon, 'Old Glenbucket', was a notable Jacobite.

Glenochar Bastel House, Lanarkshire (P)
The ruin of a fortified farm house, built about 1590, and one of a number recently discovered in the Upper Clydesdale area. The excavations have uncovered remains of numerous other dwellings, byres and enclosures, all part of the ferm toun.

Greenknowe Tower, Berwickshire (HS)
A pleasing L-plan tower house built by James Seton in 1581, added to in the following century but largely restored to its original condition in the 1930s.

Kellie Castle, Fife (NTS)
A much-altered castle, lovingly restored by the Lorimer family in the late nineteenth century. The interior has many fine features, including some superb seventeenth-century plastered ceilings.

MacLellan's Castle, Kirkcudbrightshire (HS)
An unusual, and unusually large, tower house in the centre of Kirkcudbright begun by Sir Thomas MacLellan about 1577 but never finished. The handsome monumental tomb of Sir Thomas and his second wife, Grissel Maxwell, is in the adjacent Greyfriars' Church.

Muness Castle, Shetland (HS)
The most northerly castle in the British Isles, built by Laurence Bruce in 1598. The rectangular building has round towers at diagonally opposite corners.

Noltland Castle, Orkney (HS)
A fine Z-plan tower house, built between 1560 and 1573 by Gilbert Balfour but never completed. Noted for its extravagant array of gunholes.

Scalloway Castle, Shetland (HS)
A fine tower house built in 1600 for Patrick Stewart, earl of Orkney, who was notorious for his cruelty.

Slacks Tower, Roxburghshire (P)
A rare survival of a fortified farmhouse that was once common throughout the Border country. Built by the Olivers, a noted reiving family, it is surrounded by a remarkable array of other farm buildings, all surviving as foundations only.

Further reading

Background history

Anderson, J. (ed.) *The Orkneyinga Saga*, Edinburgh, 1873 (reprinted 1990).

Barrow, G. W. S. *Kingship and unity: Scotland 1000–1306*, London, 1989.

Donaldson, Gordon *Scotland: James V – James VII*, Edinburgh, 1968.

Duncan, A. A. M. *Scotland: the making of the kingdom*, Edinburgh, 1975.

Fraser, G. M. *The Steel Bonnets*, London, 1971.

Grant, Alexander *Independence and nationhood: Scotland 1306–1469*, London, 1984.

Lynch, Michael *Scotland: a new history*, London, 1991.

Nicholson, Ranald *Scotland: the later Middle Ages*, Edinburgh, 1974.

Wormald, Jenny *Court, kirk and community: Scotland 1470–1625*, London, 1981.

Scottish castles

A considerable number of Scottish castles are in the care of Historic Scotland, and guide books are available for most of them. Detailed descriptions of many more are also to be found in the county *Inventories* of the Royal Commission on the Ancient and Historical Monuments of Scotland and *The Buildings of Scotland* series published by Penguin Books.

Caldwell, David H. (ed.) *Scottish weapons and fortifications 1100–1800*, Edinburgh, 1981.

Cruden, Stewart *The Scottish castle*, 3rd edn, Edinburgh, 1981.

Dunbar, John G. *The architecture of Scotland*, London, 1978.

Fawcett, Richard *The architectural history of Scotland from the accession of the Stewarts to the Reformation 1371–1560*, Edinburgh, 1994.

Fawcett, Richard *Stirling Castle*, London, 1995.

Howard, Deborah *Scottish architecture from the Reformation to the Restoration 1560–1660*, Edinburgh, 1995.

Lindsay, Maurice *The castles of Scotland*, London, 1986.

MacGibbon, David & Ross, Thomas *The castellated and domestic architecture of Scotland from the twelfth to the eighteenth century*, 5 vols, Edinburgh, 1887–92.

MacIvor, Iain 'Artillery and major places of strength in the Lothians and the East Border, 1513–1542', in Caldwell, David H. (ed.) *Scottish weapons and fortifications 1100–1800*, Edinburgh, 1981.

MacIvor, Iain *Edinburgh Castle*, London, 1993.

McKean, Charles 'Craignethan: the castle of the Bastard of Arran', *Proceedings of the Society of Antiquaries of Scotland*, vol. 125, 1995.

MacKenzie, William M. *The medieval castle in Scotland*, Edinburgh, 1927.

McNeill, Tom *Castles*, London, 1992.

Maxwell-Irving, A. M. T. 'Early firearms and their influence on the military and domestic architecture of the Borders', *Proceedings of the Society of Antiquaries of Scotland*, vol. 103, 1970–1.

Merriman, Marcus 'The Fortresses in Scotland', in Colvin, H. M. (ed.), *The history of the King's works, vol. IV, 1485–1660* (part II), London, 1982.

Miket, Roger & Roberts, D. L. *The mediaeval castles of Skye & Lochalsh*, Portree, 1990.

Sanderson, Margaret '"Kin, freindis and servandis", the men who worked with Archbishop David Beaton', *Innes Review*, vol. XXV, 1, 1974.

Simpson, W. Douglas *The earldom of Mar*, Aberdeen, 1949.

Simpson, G. G. & Webster, A. B. 'Charter evidence and the distribution of mottes in Scotland', *Chateau Gaillard*, vol. 5, 1970.

Stell, Geoffrey 'Architecture: the changing needs of society', in Brown, Jennifer M. (ed.) *Scottish society in the fifteenth century*, London, 1977.

Stell, Geoffrey 'Late medieval defences in Scotland', in Caldwell, David H. (ed.) *Scottish weapons and fortifications 1100–1800*, Edinburgh, 1981.

Stell, Geoffrey 'The Scottish medieval castle: form, function & evolution', in Stringer, K. J. (ed.) *Essays on the nobility in Scotland*, Edinburgh, 1985.

Tabraham, Christopher J. & Good, George L. 'The artillery fortification at Threave Castle, Galloway', in Caldwell, David H. (ed.) *Scottish weapons and fortifications 1100–1800*, Edinburgh, 1981.

Tabraham, Christopher J. 'The Scottish medieval towerhouse as lordly residence in the light of recent excavation', *Proceedings of the Society of Antiquaries of Scotland*, vol. 118, 1988.

Tabraham, Chris & Grove, Doreen *Fortress Scotland and the Jacobites*, London, 1995.

Tranter, Nigel G. *The fortified house in Scotland*, 5 vols, Edinburgh, 1962.

Zeune, Joachim *The last Scottish castles*, Buch am Erlbach, 1992.

Excavation reports

Apted, M. R. 'Excavations at Kildrummy Castle, Aberdeenshire, 1952–62', *Proceedings of the Society of Antiquaries of Scotland*, vol. 96, 1962–3.

Driscoll, S. & Yeoman, P. *Excavations at Edinburgh Castle, 1988–91*, Edinburgh, 1997.

Ewart, Gordon 'Excavations at Stirling Castle, 1977–78', *Post-medieval Archaeology*, vol. 14, 1980.

Ewart, Gordon *Cruggleton Castle: report on excavations 1978–1981*, Dumfries, 1985.

Good, George L. & Tabraham, Christopher J. 'Excavations at Threave Castle, Galloway, 1974–1978', *Medieval Archaeology*, vol. 25, 1981.

Good, George L. & Tabraham, Christopher J. 'Excavations at Smailholm Tower, Roxburghshire', *Proceedings of the Society of Antiquaries of Scotland*, vol. 118, 1988.

Haggarty, George & Tabraham, Christopher 'Excavation of a motte near Roberton, Clydesdale, 1979, *Transactions of the Dumfriesshire and Galloway Natural History and Antiquarian Society*, vol. 57, 1982.

Laing, L. R. & MacDonald, A. D. S. 'Excavations at Lochmaben Castle, Dumfriesshire', *Proceedings of the Society of Antiquaries of Scotland*, vol. 106, 1974–5.

Murray, H. K. & Murray, J. C. 'Excavations at Rattray, Aberdeenshire. A Scottish deserted burgh', *Medieval Archaeology*, vol. 37, 1993.

Yeoman, Peter A. 'Excavations at Castlehill of Strachan, 1980–81', *Proceedings of the Society of Antiquaries of Scotland*, vol. 114, 1984.

Glossary

ashlar: stone walling of the highest class, with blocks of regular size, perfectly squared, well faced and finely jointed.

barmkin: a stone wall, of middling strength, surrounding a tower-house castle and courtyard (possibly derived from *barbican*).

bastel-house: a fortified stone house, usually with a vaulted ground floor

bastion: the strongpoint of an artillery fortification corresponding to a projecting tower of a medieval castle or town wall. All bastions have two faces meeting at an angle, and two flanks which join the faces to the curtain walls.

bombard: an early, large and cumbersome cannon.

bretasche: a covered timber gallery, or hoard, on a castle wall, commanding the wall face below.

caponier: a covered passage across a defensive ditch through which gunners could fire on the attacking force.

casemate: originally a stone-vaulted gun emplacement, but later extended to include accommodation protected from heavy artillery.

corbel: a projection from a wall, supporting some structure.

crannog: a fortified island, generally man-made, in a loch.

crenelle: a notch in a parapet (see also *merlon*).

donjon: a strong central tower in a castle, usually housing the lord's residence but also serving as the place of last resort for the garrison.

ferm toun: a farm settlement.

feu: the right to the use of the land in return for a stipulated annual payment.

hackbut: an old form of hand-gun.

hammer beam: a horizontal timber, in place of a tie-beam, at or near the feet of a pair of roof rafters.

haugh, haughland: a riverside meadow or flat.

jamb: the side of any opening, such as that of a door, window or fireplace.

laigh: the Scots word for *low* or *lower*.

machicolation: a permanent stone defence at the top of a castle wall, carried on corbels (see above) with spaces in between through which the defenders could fire on their assailants below.

merlon: the solid part of a parapet between two crenelles (see above).

peel: a timber palisaded enclosure.

putlog: a cross-piece in a timber scaffolding, the inner end resting in a hole (*putlog hole*) in the wall.

ravelin: a detached triangular artillery work surrounded by its own ditch built in front of a curtain, generally at the entrance.

reiver: one who thieves or robs.

scale-and-platt stair: a stair with straight flights and landings.

yett: a grilled iron gate, placed either in front of or, more usually, behind a timber entrance door.

Index

The author

Chris Tabraham is a Principal Inspector of Ancient Monuments with Historic Scotland. A self-confessed 'castle buff', he has directed excavations at several Scottish castles and written extensively about many others.

Series editor: Dr David J. Breeze
Chief Inspector of Ancient Monuments,
Historic Scotland